SERVING WITH INTEGRITY:

THE IDEOLOGY AND PRAXIS OF SENATOR AYO FASANMI IN NIGERIAN POLITICS

By

OROBOLA FASEHUN
OLUFUNMILAYO FASEHUN

HALLARD
PRESS

Published by Hallard Press LLC.
www.HallardPress.com   Info@HallardPress.com   352-234-6099
Bulk copies of this book can be ordered at Info@HallardPress.com

Publisher's Cataloging-in-Publication data

Names: Fasehun, Orobola, author. | Fasehun, Olufunmilayo, author.
Title: Serving with integrity : the ideology and praxis of Senator Ayo Fasanmi in
Nigerian politics / Dr. Orobola Fasehun and Dr. Olufunmilayo Fasehun
Description: The Villages, FL: Hallard Press, 2022.
Identifiers: LCCN: 2022905037 | ISBN: 978-1-951188-50-4
Subjects: LCSH Fasanmi , Ayo. | Statesmen--Nigeria--Biography. | Politi-
cians--Nigeria--Biography. | Nigeria--Biography. | BIOGRAPHY & AUTOBIOG-
RAPHY / Political | BISAC BIOGRAPHY & AUTOBIOGRAPHY / Cultural, Ethnic
& Regional / African American & Black | POLITICAL SCIENCE / World / African
POLITICAL SCIENCE / Religion, Politics & State
Classification: LCC DT515.82 .F37 F47 2022 | DDC 328.669/092--dc23

Printed in the United States of America   1

ISBN: 978-1-951188-50-4 (Paperback)
ISBN: 978-1-951188-57-3 (Ebook)

HALLARD
PRESS

DEDICATION

In loving memory of

Senator Ayo Fasanmi
(September 27, 1925 - July 29, 2020)

and

Chief (Mrs.) Felicia Adejoke Fasanmi
(June 27, 1932 - October 9, 2014)

TABLE OF CONTENTS

PREFACE

This book was planned before the passing of Senator Ayo Fasanmi. We had planned to assemble and analyse the statements he made as a Member of Parliament in the First Republic (1963-1966) and, later as a Senator in the Second Republic (1979-1983).

Chief Fasanmi facilitated our task by giving us a copy of the book written on him by Akindeji Olorunyolemi and Tunde Ajibare: *Ayo Fasanmi: His Life, His Struggle* (2000). He also mentioned another book written by three authors, Yomi Ogunsanya, Stephen Gbadamosi, Bamise Jegede (2013): *By Grace: The Life and Times of Ayo Fasanmi in Politics* which he told us then needed editorial revision. We consulted these books to complement the interviews we conducted with Senator Fasanmi over several years.

In the course of our research, we made determined efforts to access the relevant Hansard (official verbatim) reports of the House of Representatives and of the Senate of the First and Second Republics respectively. Our request was directed to the Clerk of the National Assembly. Regrettably, there was no response from him. We also tried to contact the National Library in Ibadan and Abuja but there were no replies to our inquiries. We, therefore, had no option other than to extract Senator Ayo Fasanmi's statements in legislative houses from the books already written on him.

This book is divided into four chapters. Chapter One is an account of Senator Fasanmi's political biography. It delves, briefly, into his background and the political socialisation which led him to democratic socialist ideology. By ideology, we mean a belief system and guide to actions while praxis is defined as practice.

We examine his activism in the Action Group and his election to various political posts ranging from the position of Local Government Councilor to the exalted position of Senator in Nigeria's Second Republic. He was one of the few politicians in Nigeria to have served at different levels of government.

We present, in Chapter Two, a record, verbatim, of some of the statements he made at different times in the House of Representatives and the Senate of Nigeria in the years he served in those bodies.

For a full understanding and appreciation of the politics and activities of Chief Ayo Fasanmi, we have selected some of his interventions mostly by way of correspondence to his party or elected public officials. These statements and letters show his concern and advocacy of policies which he believed will benefit the masses. These statements and letters form Chapter Three of the book.

Chapter Four, which is the concluding chapter, is a selection from the numerous tributes paid to him upon his passing. These tributes acknowledge his integrity and exemplary life.

We are convinced, in writing this book, that it should be of value to Nigerians for several reasons. We mention just two. First, it should demonstrate to the discerning Nigerian reader of the book that, while most politicians go into politics for self-enrichment and wealth accumulation, there are still some Nigerians who go into politics truly to serve. Senator Fasanmi and several others in his generation served with integrity. They did not wax fat in the house of patronage nor did they use their positions to enrich themselves or family members.

A second value of the book, we like to note, is the brief historical perspective it throws on the politics of pre-independence and post-independence Nigeria. The book also examines, in passing, the consequences of military rule, a major one of which is the clearly truncated federalism we are currently saddled with in the country.

It is our hope that the vision of Senator Ayo Fasanmi for a developed and truly federal Nigeria that is egalitarian and where corruption is tamed will be achieved.

Orobola Fasehun, Ph.D
Olufunmilayo Fasehun, Ph.D

March 2022

Orobola Fasehun & Olufunmilayo Fasehun

ACKNOWLEDGEMENTS

Growing up in the Fasanmi household, we led such a normal life that it was hard to tell that we had an activist father. We had no fancy house or big car. If there was any TV appearance by father, he took the whole family in his Volkswagen to a friend's house to watch it on black and white TV. Senator Ayo Fasanmi and wife lived frugally but had lots of love and laughs to share with their family, friends and neighbours.

Although Senator Fasanmi wore many hats, to his family he was simply a decent and good family man. He was caring, amiable and loving. He would not go to bed until everyone in his household had been accounted for. He once chartered a taxi from Osogbo to Iwo in Osun State to pick up his sick daughter from school.

My mother, Chief (Mrs.) Felicia Adejoke Fasanmi, was his sweetheart and soul mate. In her, he found a wife that was totally committed to his ideology and politics. Father's friends and political associates, no matter what time of the day they showed up at our door, were always welcome and entertained.

When my mother took ill in 2010, father fed her, supervised her caregivers, and stayed by her side, day and night, until she passed away on October 9, 2014.

Senator Fasanmi was equally nice to those who worked for him. I remember a security guard, who worked for him for many years, was treated like a member of our family. When he passed away, father was responsible for all the funeral expenses. He was a benefactor to a lot of people.

Father and I were professional colleagues as both of us were trained as pharmacists. I was very proud of him when he was elected President of the Pharmaceutical Society of Nigeria, and later a Fellow of the same Society.

Senator Fasanmi became a devout Christian later in life and a member of both the Anglican Church, Agoro, Osogbo and St John's Anglican Church, Iye-Ekiti.

As a politician, the Senator had quite a number of political associates with some of whom he became quite close during his over seven decades in politics. Some of them considered him as their political father or mentor.

I am profoundly grateful to former Governors - Chief Bisi Akande, Asiwaju Bola Tinubu, Niyi Adebayo, and Ogbeni Rauf Aregbesola - as well as serving Governors, Kayode Fayemi and Adegboyega Oyetola. Governors Kayode Fayemi, Adegboyega Oyetola and Asiwaju Bola Tinubu were particularly helpful in his last years and took care of him during his sickness. They also assisted in several ways including during his obsequies. They were like biological sons to him.

I am beholden to Governor Fayemi for honouring my father by naming a Model College after him, for his contributions to

Ekiti State. Unfortunately, the Senator passed away before the college was commissioned.

To the Kabiyesis, the Oniye of Iye Ekiti, Oba Jonathan Adeleye-Oni, Ilufemiloye I, and the Ataoja of Osogbo, Oba Jimoh Oyetunji Olanipekun, Laroye II, I express appreciation to them for their unflinching moral support of my father. Equally, I thank Alayemore of Ido Osun, Oba Aderemi Adedapo Adeen, for showing up with his Chiefs almost every year, in the last five years of father's life, to celebrate his birthday with all pomp and pageantry.

I like to thank my wonderful siblings, Mrs. Olufunke Oluyide, Dr. Folake Olaleye, Justice Obafemi Fasanmi, and Mr. Afolabi Fasanmi and their spouses, and all the grandchildren for their unconditional love, unwavering moral support and care of parents in old age.

I acknowledge the contributions of the Fasanmi clan in Iye-Ekiti and Lagos, and my uncles and aunties for being there for my father.

Equally, I thank Mr. Temitope Adebayo, who was father's Personal Assistant for thirteen years and Mrs. Bosede Alade-Okin, a caregiver to both parents, for taking excellent care of father.

I also appreciate and thank Professors Agboola Adesanoye, Olusola Ojo and Olu Moloye who graciously read the initial manuscript and made useful editorial suggestions.

Last but not least, I would like to thank Ambassador (Dr.) Orobola Fasehun, my husband. He brought his training as a political scientist to bear by consulting with, and drafting statements for Senator Fasanmi while he was alive. Indeed, he had proposed and father had agreed before his passing for Dr. Fasehun to write Senator Fasanmi's political biography. This work, then, is a collaborative project between a daughter and son-in-law of Senator Fasanmi. It is a fitting tribute to the memory of my father, an activist, a man of flawless integrity till he passed.

Olufunmilayo Fasehun (née Fasanmi), Ph.D.

CHAPTER ONE

POLITICAL BIOGRAPHY OF SENATOR AYO FASANMI

Early years

Born of Iye-Ekiti and Ijero-Ekiti humble parentage in Lagos on September 27, 1925, Chief Ayo Fasanmi grew up to be a man of discipline, principle, and political activism for over seven decades. He was an active witness of Nigeria's transition from colonial rule to independence, as well as its praetorian guard (military) rule from 1966 to 1999 when civil rule was fully restored. A hiatus in military rule when there was a short civilian rule occurred between 1979 and 1983. Chief Fasanmi belonged to the group of prominent political actors in pre-coup and post-coup Nigeria.

At his birth in 1925, colonial Nigeria was only eleven years old, the British created state-nations having been amalgamated in 1914. The establishment of Nigeria was due to inter-imperial rivalry amongst European powers who carved Africa into colonies beholden to themselves. The division of Africa into spheres of influence decided at the infamous Berlin Conference of 1884-1885 conceded the area to be known initially as Northern and Southern Nigeria Protectorates to the United Kingdom which had been active in the area prior to the Berlin Conference. The two protectorates, the internal boundaries of which had been arbitrarily decided without regard to ethnic boundaries, were fused together in 1914 to form the dependency of Nigeria under British imperial rule.[1]

Whilst there were many reasons for the establishment of Nigeria, the desire to extract resources of the land could be said to be the foremost reason and to do this, the tragic slave trade prevalent at the time was suppressed and replaced with "legitimate" trade in raw materials, such as palm oil, cocoa and cotton which fed the growing industries of Great Britain.

The differences in the productivity of the two protectorates as well as accessibility to the coastline made the southern protectorate the prized land that generated funds for the administration of the two protectorates. The differential impact of British colonial policy on the two protectorates is still evident till date in the areas of education, economic and social development as well as political integration. Indeed, the differential is manifested in the centrifugal forces that pull Nigeria apart, and in the demand for "true" federalism.

In the 46-year period of British rule of Nigeria, there was minimal investment in education and infrastructure. When schools were established, it was largely by religious groups and local communities at primary school level. These schools were few and found in Lagos and a few major urban centres.

Secondary schools were scanty and operated by missionaries or communities.

Formal western education for young Ayo Fasanmi did not start until 1935 at St. Paul's Catholic School, Ebute Metta. While growing up, his parents, Mr. Joseph Fadahunsi Fasanmi and Mrs. Aina Oloriegbe Fasanmi (nee Erungbemika) instilled in him the importance of honesty, discipline, integrity and hard work. His father gave him practical experience of hard work by regularly taking him to work with him in his brick masonry job.

The values of probity inculcated into young Ayo were taken by him to the household he lived in, and the primary schools he attended in Ibadan (now in Oyo State), Offa (now in Kwara State), and Kafanchan (now in Kaduna State). His education at the primary school level was made possible by his uncle, Mr. Samuel Adeniyi Williams, a Nigerian railway employee, who took over the sponsorship of young Ayo's education when he dropped out of St. Paul's Catholic School due to limited financial means of his parents. Those years were also the time when the global economy was in depression. The colonial periphery, as Nigeria was then, was also severely affected as demands for raw materials, which colonial Nigeria exported to the United Kingdom, the metropole, collapsed.

His uncle, who had one of the few technical jobs available then, took Ayo to these various railway cities. Young Ayo was thus able to travel out of Yorubaland and, consequently, privileged to see and experience first-hand other parts of Nigeria beyond his Yoruba homeland. He was one of the few politicians of his age who ventured out of their homeland at a young age. This made him to be pan-Nigerian from his youth and this would be deepened when he got admitted to Government College Ibadan, in 1942, where he met many students from other parts of Nigeria.

Educational Experience and Development of his Ideology

Young Ayo's years in Government College, Ibadan, (GCI) which he attended from 1942 to 1947 on scholarship, nurtured his political beliefs as well as his anti-colonialism and nationalism stance which had started whilst he was in primary school. His nationalist feelings, in his young age, were influenced by Dr. Nnamdi Azikiwe and his newspaper, *West African Pilot*.

Chief Ayo Fasanmi, in his oral reminiscences during one of our conversations, recalled that, as a young lad, he used to attend Azikiwe's lectures at Tom Jones Hall on Lagos Island. Azikiwe's speeches were laced with anti-colonial rhetoric and demand for independence for colonial Nigeria. This, in effect, served as the beginning of his political socialisation, which would deepen further in future years.

Government College Ibadan (GCI) in the 1940s brought together many young Nigerians from the southern part of colonial Nigeria. Many of the students, like young Ayo, had been influenced by the fervour of the demand for independence. Some of his schoolmates then would later become prominent in independent Nigeria. Amongst such mates were Abiodun Aloba (1921-2001) journalist and Assistant to Prime Minister Tafawa Balewa, and President Shehu Shagari; Kolawole Balogun (1922-2002), Federal Minister of Information; and Tunji Otegbeye (1925-2009) Medical Director and Proprietor of Ireti Hospital,

Lagos, and a well-known politician.

While in GCI, young Ayo was a sportsman, food prefect and actor. His acting in a play titled *Strife* in GCI, where he played the part of a labour leader during a strike in Great Britain raised his consciousness about socioeconomic issues and the plight of workers in colonial Nigeria. The play had a huge impact on him and was the beginning of his thinking about socialism as the antidote to poverty which he reasoned was caused by capitalism.

One lasting experience young Ayo took out of Government College, Ibadan, was his life-long friendship with Tunji Otegbeye. The friendship lasted sixty-seven years until the latter died in 2009. Like Ayo, young Tunji was concerned about poverty and the welfare of the common man. The friendship morphed into sympathy for socialism as his statements during a May Day rally as well as some of his speeches in Nigerian legislative houses would later attest.

Professional Training as a Pharmacist

After graduation from GCI in 1947, young Ayo trained as a pharmacist in Yaba School of Pharmacy for three years. Thereafter, he began his career as a pharmacist-trainee in General Hospital on Broad Street, Lagos and, subsequently as a licensed pharmacist, served in different hospitals in Ibadan, Oyo and Osogbo. He withdrew from government service in 1955 and established Bamidupe Chemist in 1956 in Osogbo, a town that would serve practically as his second home for over six decades. Bamidupe Chemist was the first privately owned pharmacy in

Osogbo, and it provided pharmaceutical services to the people of Osogbo and its environs.

In his early years in Osogbo, the then reigning Ataoja Oba Samuel Adenle I, (1944-1976) in recognition of his service to Osogbo people, offered him acres of land from the rail line to Okefia. The land must have been over ten acres. Whilst thanking the Oba for the offer, he politely declined the gift. This was a clear indication of his aversion to wealth accumulation and his leaning towards socialism.

Pharmacist Fasanmi actively participated in the meetings of the Pharmaceutical Society in Oyo State and, subsequently, became Chairman of the Oyo State Chapter in 1973. He was later elected President of the Pharmaceutical Society of Nigeria (1977-1979). He became a Fellow of the Society in 1984.

As a retired pharmacist, he played an active role in the Society and from time to time hosted members of the Osun State Chapter of Pharmaceutical Society at his Osogbo residence.

Beginning of Family Life

While working as a pharmacist, he formally married his soul mate and sweetheart, Miss Felicia Adejoke Oyelade, a British trained registered nurse and midwife, in a civil marriage then followed by a church blessing service. Mama would later establish Bamidupe Maternity Home that served the people of Osogbo and its environs. The marriage produced six children, three girls and three boys. Ayo Fasanmi, Jnr, the fifth child, tragically, lost his life in a car accident in 1985. Five of the children survived him and all are university graduates in various fields such as pharmacy, nursing, civil engineering, law and geophysics. The children are Dr. Olufunmilayo Fasanmi-Fasehun, Mrs. Olufunke Fasanmi-Oluyide, Dr. Folake Fasanmi-Olaleye, Justice Obafemi Fasanmi, and Mr. Afolabi Fasanmi.

Chief (Mrs.) Felicia Adejoke Fasanmi pre-deceased her husband in 2014.

Formal Entry into Politics

Chief Fasanmi's withdrawal from government service in 1955 enabled him to devote more of his time to politics. To enhance his credentials and capacity, he planned to study law like many in his generation who were in politics, but the plan fell through due to family obligations.

The main political issue when he aspired to be a lawyer was the agitation for independence for colonial Nigeria. The three political parties that were the major actors in the constitutional negotiations for independence were the welfarist-oriented Action Group (AG), the liberal National Council of Nigerian Citizens (NCNC), and the conservative Northern People's Congress (NPC). Each party dominated the region of its leader. Thus, the Action Group under Chief Obafemi Awolowo was dominant in the Western Region, the National Council of Nigerian Citizens led by Dr. Nnamdi Azikiwe drew most of its support from Eastern Region and a few urban areas in the West whilst the Northern People's Congress, as its name indicates, enjoyed unequalled dominance in the Northern Region, to which it restricted its political activities.

The constitution which was agreed by the leaders in 1957 was a federal constitution, even though during the negotiation for independence various views had been expressed as to what should be the political structure of independent Nigeria. These views ranged from unitary state, a preference of some supporters of the NCNC, to suggestions for a federal system advocated by Awolowo and Ahmadu Bello. Strong regional autonomy had been one of the objectives of the Northern People's Congress.

The agreed constitution endorsed the tripodal political structure, which the British colonial authorities had imposed on Nigeria in 1939 when it divided the Southern provinces into Eastern and Western Provinces, which were later named regions while the Northern Protectorate, twice the land size of the Southern provinces, was left intact. The inherent instability in that structure would later manifest itself, a few years after independence, with far-reaching consequences for the country. That inglorious inheritance has remained an albatross around the neck of Nigeria up till this day.

Chief Fasanmi was initially not a member of any of the political parties that agitated for independence. However, his predisposition to fight poverty and to help the common man caused him to share the same vision with the Action Group. In his student days in Government College, he had been a member of the Zikist Movement and had, in fact, written newspaper articles for the *West African Pilot* of Dr. Nnamdi Azikiwe. However, the party programme of the Action Group as well as its organisation was attractive to him. The most important factor that lured him into the Action Group, however, according to him was the activism of the party and its leader, Awolowo, whom in later years, he described as "the greatest schemer and planner ever."

Chief Fasanmi formally joined the Action Group after a formal invitation to him by Chief Awolowo. The invitation had been preceded by a May Day rally in which he had publicly declared that he was an independent member of the Action Group. That statement had led to a meeting with Chief Awolowo in which the latter had asked him to clarify the statement: "independent Action Group member". Fasanmi replied that "if the party does what is right, I will support it; on the other hand, if it does what is wrong, I will oppose it, since I am not a card-carrying member." Thereafter, he was invited to join the party.[2]

Activities in the Action Group

In his years in the Action Group, Chief Fasanmi served in different capacities, beginning with his election as the leader of the Action Group Youth Association in 1962 after the defection of Chief Remi Fanimokun-Kayode to the NCNC. He was also a member of the National Reconciliation Committee. The Committee was a policy think-tank for the party which produced several policy papers that were debated, amended and then agreed.

If the majority agreed on the policy recommendations in the paper whatever the reservations of the party leader, Chief Awolowo, that majority position became the Action Group position and that position was defended publicly by Chief Awolowo. Other members of the Reconciliation Committee were Sam Aluko (1929-2012), S.G Ikoku (1922-1997), Bola Ige (1930-2001), and Bisi Onabanjo (1927-1990). These young men were the ones who, in their policy papers, pushed for the adoption of democratic socialism as the ideology of the Action Group. It is indeed reasonable to argue that the party slogan of "Life More Abundant" was folded into the liberal democratic socialism of the party.

The liberal democratic socialism of the Action Group, including belief in regular, free and fair elections, was different from the scientific socialism of Karl Marx, who interpreted history as a class struggle between the property owning class and workers, with the eventual overthrow of the bourgeoisie, the capital-owning class, by the proletariat, that is, the workers.

The ideology of the Action Group was one of the reasons cited by the dissidents for pulling out of the party in 1962. The dissidents led by Chief S.L. Akintola, then Deputy Leader of the Action Group, hurriedly formed an alliance with NCNC to enable Akintola, who was then the Premier of the Western Region, to continue his rule. However, the majority of Action Group members and most people of the Western Region remained loyal to Chief Awolowo.

Many of the Action Group members who remained loyal to Chief Awolowo and the party faced severe political persecution. They were detained on false charges and harassed by thugs. Chief Fasanmi was one of the members of the party that bore the brunt of the oppression. He was detained many times and was, on one occasion, tear-gassed in the residence of Chief Awolowo in Ibadan. Thugs were also mobilized against him. However, he did not waver despite the oppression and entreaties to him by Chief Akintola to switch parties. He stayed loyal to the Action Group, its leader and its ideology. It was clearly his belief in Chief Awolowo and the ideology of the party that made him testify in Awolowo's defence, when the latter was tried for treason in 1963.

Chief Ayo Fasanmi remained steadfast in his support of Chief Awolowo despite the latter's incarceration. Not only did Chief Fasanmi visit him in detention at Lekki in 1962, he was a regular contributor to the *Nigerian Tribune,* a newspaper owned by Chief Awolowo. In his essays in the *Nigerian Tribune*, he wrote trenchantly about Nigerian politics expressing his views on various political issues. This was from 1965 to 1967.

Elections into Political Offices

Throughout the period of electoral politics from pre-independence to 1966, and from 1979 to 1983, Chief Fasanmi was elected to several legislative bodies beginning at the local government to the highest law-making body in Nigeria in 1979, the Senate of the Federal Republic.

His first contest was to the Ijero Local Government in 1959 which he won. In 1964, he was elected to the Federal Parliament under the Action Group, which was then a member of the United Progressive Grand Alliance (UPGA), an alliance between the National Council of Nigerian Citizens (NCNC), and the Northern Elements Progressive Union (NEPU). Many left-of-centre parties were also in the Alliance.

In the initial phase of the Obasanjo military transition to

civilian rule in 1978, Chief Ayo Fasanmi contested for the post of Councillor and won election to Ido Osi Local Government. He was also a member of the 1977 Constituent Assembly which debated the draft 1979 Constitution of Nigeria.

In 1979, he contested election to the Senate of the Federal Republic under the banner of the Unity Party of Nigeria (UPN), a successor political party to the Action Group. The leader of the UPN was Chief Obafemi Awolowo, his political mentor. Chief Fasanmi won that election, becoming a Senator in the Second Republic of Nigeria, and won re-election in 1983 representing the then Ondo North Senatorial Constituency.

His contest in the primary of the UPN to be the candidate of the party for Ondo State governorship election in 1979 did not succeed. His main opponent was the elderly Chief Michael Ajasin (1908-1997), who was one of the founders of the Action Group. Chief Ajasin prevailed in the party primary and was subsequently elected as the civilian Governor of Ondo State, which then included four Ekiti Divisions. In 1996, the four Divisions became Ekiti State.

Chief Fasanmi's rate of high electoral success was due to several factors. First, was his populist style. He reached out to all regardless of income or background and welcomed many people to his homes in Osogbo and Iye-Ekiti. In most cases, his guests were treated to nice meals.

A second reason was his generosity. Out of his means, he assisted several people to be educated as well as secure employment. One example out of several was the sponsorship of his newspaper vendor who, though a brilliant young man, lacked the means to pursue higher education. Chief Fasanmi paid for his university education. Several others from his constituency in Ekiti were assisted through secondary to higher education also.

A third reason for Chief Fasanmi's popularity was his honesty. There was not a whiff of corruption in him; his integrity was impeccable. Indeed, he was considered a genuine clean "Man of the People."

Service in Federal Legislative Houses

Legislatures in liberal democratic systems are forums for their members to express matters of concern to their constituents, their party and the nation. They can also lobby for or sponsor private members' bills in a presidential form of government.

Nigeria, since independence, has had a truly unfettered legislature for only 27 years. Elected legislatures without military overlord functioned from 1960 to 1966 and from 1999 till the time of writing. Though there were legislatures under the rule of Babangida, their decisions were often circumscribed and compromised.

Chief Fasanmi served in Federal legislatures two times: first as a member of the Federal House of Representatives (1964-1966); and, second, as a Senator in the Senate (1979-1983).

In the Senate, he was a member of two committees, Health and Social Services, and Public Works. He spoke on several issues relating to his assignments, as well as on other important matters that were of concern to him and that reflected his belief system.[3]

The No-Politics of Praetorian Guard Rule

In six decades of Nigeria's independence, the military ruled the country for a period of 28 years during which it banned party politics except in the transition phases to civilian rule.

Several reasons were given for military intrusion into politics.[4] There were allegations of corruption against politicians, and mismanagement of the economy by ruling civilian elites. To these reasons should be added intra-military rivalry due to ethnic or regional competition as well as ambition of top military rulers. The lasting impact of military rule on Nigeria is an over-centralized, unitary state dressed in the garb of federalism, in which clientelist politics is dominant.[5] That indeed is the legacy of military political engineering in Nigeria.

During its rule of Nigeria, the military appropriated to itself executive and legislative functions and it co-opted politicians, academics and business executives to head the ministries or parastatals.

Chief Fasanmi was one of the politicians of the First Republic to head a parastatal, owing largely to his integrity. He was appointed by Governor Oluwole Rotimi to serve as a Director of the Western Nigeria Housing Corporation. He served from 1972 to 1975. The Corporation was in charge of estates and lands in areas of high value such as Ikeja in Lagos and Bodija Estate in Ibadan. Given his discipline and opposition to corruption, he did not enrich himself or family members by awarding himself or relatives land allocations in the then Western State which included the current states of Ekiti, Ogun, Ondo, Osun and Oyo.

This aversion to corruption led him to create a non-governmental organisation in 1972, the Anti-Bribery and Corruption Committee, which later became the National Anti-Bribery and Corruption Commission which had the support of the then Commissioner of Police in charge of Criminal Investigation Department of the Nigerian Police in Lagos, Mr. Sunday Adewusi.

Chief Ayo Fasanmi and the Travails of Democracy in Nigeria

During the regime of General Ibrahim Babangida, a political bureau created by the General made several recommendations regarding Nigeria's political future. Some of these recommendations were adopted by the Armed Forces Ruling Council and this laid the foundation for gradual transition to civil rule under the self-styled military president, Major General Ibrahim Babangida.

The transition was occasionally halted and characterised by ban and unbanning of politicians. Ultimately, election to the office of President was held in June 1993 between the two parties earlier created by Babangida: the Social Democratic Party, said to be left-of-centre, and the counterpart, the right leaning National Republican Convention. The victor in the election was the left-of-centre party candidate, the rich philanthropist, Chief Moshood Kashimawo Abiola. However, through judicial shenanigans orchestrated by General Babangida and the "militicians", that is, military men who were really politicians in uniform, the election was annulled.

Domestic and international pressures on Babangida forced

him to "step aside" (to use his own words) in August 1993. He then appointed Mr. Ernest Shonekan, a lawyer and businessman, to replace him, to prepare yet another transition programme. Mr. Shonekan was sacked from office by Major General Sani Abacha after a court case that nullified Shonekan's appointment. Like Babangida, Abacha was a career coup plotter who participated in the coup that overthrew President Shehu Shagari in 1983 and supported Babangida when the latter sacked Major General Muhammdu Buhari as military Head of State of Nigeria in August 1985.

The annulment of the June 12, 1993 election of Abiola as President of the Federal Republic of Nigeria led to the formation of a strong civil society coalition of pro-democracy organisation, the National Democracy Coalition (NADECO). The aim of the coalition was to pressure the military for the installation of Abiola as President of Nigeria. Prominent members of NADECO included old politicians who had been in the Action Group such as Chief Michael Ajasin, Chief Abraham Adesanya and Chief Ayo Fasanmi. Younger elements in the coalition were Ahmed Bola Tinubu, Dr Kayode Fayemi, and Professor Ropo Sekoni.

In November 1993, General Abacha dissolved the political structure of the inappropriately named Third Republic which he had inherited from Babangida and which he had endorsed as Army Chief of Staff and member of the Armed Forces Ruling Council. Abacha followed the announcement of the dissolution by unfolding his plan for a Constitutional Conference that would decide on yet another constitution for Nigeria. Chief Fasanmi heard on radio in June 1994 that he had been nominated as a member of the panel that would organise the conference. After consulting with his political associates, he accepted the appointment.

When the panel began its meeting, Chief Fasanmi withdrew from the panel and gave reasons for his resignation, though he knew there would be certain risks to his freedom and person. The first reason was that certain draft provisions in the constitution were bound to compromise the secular nature of Nigeria. A second reason was the self-succession plan of Abacha which was being pushed by his sycophants in the conference. Indeed, Chief Fasanmi was offered a bribe ostensibly to support the self-succession scheme. The final reason was the call of Yoruba leaders for all Yoruba participants to withdraw from the conference.

The death of Abacha on June 8, 1998 ended his self-succession manoeuvre. His successor, Major General Abdulsalami Abubakar, began a new transition plan which allowed the formation of political parties.

Formation of the Alliance for Democracy and other Progressive Parties

Alliance for Democracy, a major political party in Nigeria, until it fused with other parties to transform into the Action Congress of Nigeria and, subsequently, the All Progressives Congress, was one of the parties formed when, yet again, the military permitted the formation of political parties. The party, which was formed in the residence of Chief Fasanmi in Osogbo, brought together many politicians who had been members of the Action Group (1951-1966) and the Unity Party of Nigeria (1978-

1983). The party had its base in the South-West from which it drew enormous political support.

Chief Fasanmi was elected Vice Chairman of Alliance for Democracy for the South-West of Nigeria. The ideology of the party was described as "progressivism", with emphasis on the welfare policies of its predecessor political parties, the Action Group and the Unity Party of Nigeria.

The candidates of the Alliance for Democracy in the 1999 elections won the governorship posts in South-West States: Ekiti (Adeniyi Adebayo), Lagos (Bola Tinubu), Ogun (Segun Osoba), Ondo (Adebayo Adefarati), Oyo (Lam Adesina) and Osun (Bisi Akande). Chief Fasanmi had strongly supported all the above-named gubernatorial candidates including that of his state, Adeniyi Adebayo. He would later give the same level of support to Dr. Kayode Fayemi in his two contests for the governorship of Ekiti State in 2010 and 2018.

Chief Fasanmi also supported, through public statements and endorsements, several other candidates of the All Progessives Congress in 2015 following the merger of a number of parties to form the party. His public support and endorsement of Muhammed Buhari in 2015, no doubt contributed to the election of Buhari as president in 2015.

Chief Fasanmi was also active in Egbe Afenifere, the Yoruba socio-cultural group that was the backbone of the Alliance for Democracy. When the Egbe had fissures in 2008 following the death of its leader, Chief Abraham Adesanya, Chief Ayo Fasanmi was approached to be the leader of Egbe Afenifere Renewal Group.

Conclusion

In his years in politics, beginning as a militant student nationalist to his election as a legislator on the platform of progressive parties, the Action Group (AG) and the Unity Party of Nigeria (UPN) and, subsequently, as elder statesman, Chief Ayo Fasanmi displayed certain impressive and noteworthy attributes. He served with integrity, displayed unwavering loyalty to progressive parties, and lived a simple life consistent with his ideology of democratic socialism. He, thus, flawlessly blended his belief with practice.

Chief Fasanmi was in the league of those who sought and, to a large extent, transformed the South-West of Nigeria in the early 1960s to be the leading region in Nigeria in terms of education, infrastructure development as well as medical services. The transformation was due to the vision, discipline and inspiration earlier provided by the Action Group under its historic and iconic leader, Chief Obafemi Awolowo.

Until his passing in July 2020, Chief Fasanmi, together with many others in his generation displayed exemplary qualities, bringing into public service a commitment that has not been matched. The sterling qualities of that generation should be the template for fashioning a restructured Nigeria. Nigerian leaders should be transformative, following the pattern of Chief Awolowo, Lee Kuan Yew of Singapore, and Seretse Khama of Botswana. The latter country is ranked as "the least corrupt in Africa", a fact that would have gladdened the heart of Chief Fasanmi, a lifelong champion of probity in governance and a true "man of the people".

CHAPTER TWO

STATEMENTS IN THE HOUSE OF REPRESENTATIVES AND SENATE

In this chapter Chief Fasanmi's Statements made in the House of Representatives between 1964-1966, and later in the Senate from 1979-1983 are presented. The speeches covered a variety of issues which were topical in Nigeria then, and some of which are still relevant today.

STATEMENTS IN THE HOUSE OF REPRESENTATIVES

We begin with his statement made in the House of Representatives in March 1965. The statement was made in response to the speech of the then non-executive President, Honourable Dr. Nnamdi Azikiwe. Below is a verbatim account of Chief Fasanmi's statement.

Urgent issues facing the nation

"The people of this country are very anxious that the constitution of this country be reviewed as soon as possible. I know how some people are fighting shy of a review of the constitution because if any progressive review is made it will jeopardise their chances of ruling a section of the country. I am here referring to the NNDP.

An immediate review of our constitution is a dire necessity if we are to preserve the corporate existence and unity of Nigeria.

The conduct of the last election was a mockery of democracy, and by the entire exercise we have shown very glaringly that the ballot box was becoming discredited. As a result, we have in this House, members who are not true representatives of their people. The entire electoral machinery must be overhauled immediately in order to ensure free and fair elections all over the country. Towards this end, it is very necessary that the local government police and Native Authority Police should be brought directly under the control of the Inspector General of Police. At the moment, the local government police and the Native Authority Police have become a veritable instrument of oppression in the hands of politicians who want to remain in power at all costs.

As I was saying, at the moment, the local government police and the Native Authority Police have become instruments of oppression in the hands of politicians who want to remain in power at all costs against the popular will of the people. Also, the powers of the customary courts and the Alkali courts must be limited strictly to customary matters instead of being used as a political weapon against political opponents.

The President's speech made no mention of the cankerworm of tribalism which is destroying the fabric of our society. I must say that tribalism has become a pragmatic instrument of national destruction and disunity. Events of recent times, and they are many, too many to recount, have made it necessary for the government to legislate on tribalism.

Therefore, I should also like to suggest that in the interest of national unity, the Northern People's Congress should be thinking of changing its name from a regional party to a national one. After all, the foster child of the NPC, the NNDP, in spite of its tribalistic tendencies, has changed its name to the Nigerian National Democratic Party in spite of the fact that it is neither Nigerian, it is neither national nor is it democratic; and it is not a party. It is a club of conspirators and carpet crossers.

In the President's speech, it is said that the Government will encourage a greater amount of overseas investment in the tin mining industry. May I say that in a major industry like tin mining, the tendency should be towards public ownership or at the worst, the concentration of ownership should tilt in favour of Nigerian indigenes.

As I was saying, in a major industry like tin mining, the tendency should be towards public ownership instead of encouraging overseas investors to flood the market. In this respect, I would like to suggest that miners should be given adequate protection and that the wages paid to them should be enough to keep body and soul together.

I am very happy to hear from the President's speech that efforts will be made to establish iron and steel industries in this country. I am happy that there is a project of this nature going on in the North and the East. I hope that within a short space of time, the Government will consider the possibility of having the same project in the West.

In the President's speech, it was said that the Government will pursue a policy of non-alignment. As far as the progressive elements of this country are concerned, the foreign policy of the government is only non-aligned on paper. It is not non-aligned in practice. I am saying this because people from the socialist countries are strictly restricted in coming into this country whereas people from Britain, Germany and other Western countries are given unlimited facilities of bringing in people into this country.

Attempts should be made to establish an embassy in Israel. If Israel can come to establish an embassy here, I do not see the reason why we should not establish one in Israel. The question of religion should not prevent us from establishing an embassy in Israel".

Advocacy for Socialism and Nationalism for Economic Development

In a speech made in the House of Representatives on April 3, 1965, Chief Fasanmi defended socialism as he prayed that God should give Nigeria "men of integrity... who are truly dedicated to the ideals of pragmatic and democratic socialism."

Following is the full statement:
"In the lengthy preamble to the Budget speech, this House

was treated to a new anti-socialist doctrine based on political and economic heresies. If I may borrow his words, the Minister said, among other things, that socialism means a complete subordination of individual freedom to the supposed interest of the State. May I say that individuals make up the States and power actually resides in them. The interest of the people is supreme, and the State relies on the joint and cooperative activities of individuals for the essential material ingredients of living.

Furthermore, the basic principle of any society is the subordination of individual freedom to the interest of the State. May I ask, if socialism is un-Nigerian and a violation of the Constitution, why must it, therefore, constitute an anathema to some people? Surely the freedom that is being advocated is not the freedom by a Minister to run a privileged and protected industry just because our brand of capitalism knows no code of conduct.

Talking of nationalisation, why are some people scared stiff of the word "nationalisation"? In his speech, the Minister of Finance said that since we value our personal freedom very highly, nationalisation must be completely unacceptable to all true and honest Nigerians. May I again ask: What is wrong with the nationalisation of, say, the tin mining industry, petroleum industry, banking and insurance businesses? These institutions constitute the pride of the nation which must not be left in the hands of foreign monopolistic capitalists. Their nationalisation must, therefore, be acceptable to all true and honest Nigerians who cherish the economic freedom of the nation.

The Minister in his speech calls for sacrifice by asking every one of us to set aside part of the fruits of today's labour for tomorrow. This is an excellent idea, but may I ask, what sacrifice does the Minister expect the common man to make? The Minister regrets that the Nigerian public has not shown ready response to previous calls for national savings. What does the Minister expect the people to do—people who have not got enough to eat, people who only live from hand to mouth? And in any case, we have not lived a life of rededication which the Minister was preaching, which will serve as a shining example to the people who look forward to us for succour and guidance.

As I said, how would the Minister go out and tell people to come and make sacrifices when in this House out of every five members of the House, one is a Minister of State! What exactly would the Minister want from the people? The Government should have shown a better example if, instead of creating about eighty ministerial posts, they created about thirty ministerial posts and, instead of paying fabulous allowances to Ministers and Parliamentary Secretaries, they should have given an example of austerity.

In his Budget speech, the Minister said, and with your permission, Mr. Speaker, I quote 'increased productivity in the farm must go hand in hand with industrialisation, and I think that the most fruitful approach to the problem lies in the encouragement of farm settlement.'

May I say that farm settlement is more of an experimental venture more than anything else. I would like to suggest to the Minister that we should direct our attention to something in form of cooperative farming and state farming.

I just like to say a word or two on the question of petroleum industry in this country. In the Budget speech, the Minister painted a very bright and rosy picture of our earnings on petroleum. With your permission, I want to quote the Minister's speech which says:

'Hitherto, the Shell-BP Petroleum Development Company of Nigeria Limited has been the only exporter of oil, but I am happy to say that already a second company, the Nigerian Gulf Oil Company, is producing and exporting oil commercially. There is every indication that these two companies will soon be joined by others in contributing to the industry's export earnings, reaching a level not less than 100 million pounds by 1967. The balance of payments situation will thus be transformed overnight.'

May I say that the petroleum industry is a very tricky business. I would like to make this humble suggestion that a parliamentary committee should be set up to investigate the revenue accruing from the oil industry and to know how much of this profit is coming to the coffers of the Government.

Finally, I would like to say something about unemployment. I think one of the social maladies that now afflict this nation is unemployment, and I would like our Government to take a more progressive measure in tackling this problem. I am sure that if the Minister is prepared to accept a socialist way of life—either progressive, pragmatic or democratic—the question of unemployment will be solved.

I would like to conclude my speech by re-emphasizing that this country and indeed, those of us who are members of this honourable House, should be really prepared to rededicate ourselves to the services of this nation. It is not only a rededication, but a rebirth of some people who do not believe in socialism. I pray that God should give us men whom the lust of office will not buy, men of honour, men of integrity, men who will not sell this nation for a pot of pottage, men who are truly dedicated to the ideals of pragmatic and democratic socialism."

STATEMENTS IN THE SENATE

1981 Appropriation Bill in the Senate

The issues that Chief Fasanmi raised in his Appropriation Bill statement on February 9, 1981—corruption, ethnicity, and poverty—are still very much with us today in Nigeria. The Senator proceeded in his speech to advise then President Shehu Shagari to be wary of sycophants and praise singers who often lead people astray. This is the statement:

"Mr. President, the 1981 Budget marks a significant milestone in the life of the Nation. In the first instance, it is the first budget ever to mark the coming into full effect of the change over to a new system in which the financial year coincides with the calendar year. The 1980 estimate covered only a period of nine months. In the second instance, it is also the first budget for which the present administration can be held to full accountability as the 1980 budget could be rightly regarded as a handover of the previous military administration.

Before Dr. K. O. Mbadiwe performs his usual ritual in christening the present budget, let me give him a helping hand so that he does not raise the President's hope unnecessarily. The

1981 Budget is a budget of despair.

I did mention that peace, progress and stability are necessary to foster and generate a healthy economy which is the cornerstone of any budgetary exercise. I must confess that I am very much apprehensive and sometimes dismayed at the growing trend of bitterness and rancour in our national life. For over three years, we fought a bloody civil war to ensure the peace, progress and stability of Nigeria. Some of the horrifying incidents which precipitated the holocaust are again rearing their ugly heads. Once again, we are ensnared in the web of corruption, trapped so cleverly and almost completely that we can no longer see either the cause or the evil that is inflicting such deadly pain on our society.

In the second instance, some of our leaders from all sides of the country in the attempt to promote personal gain and selfish interests and aggrandizements, are back at the old game of inciting passions, creating disaffections and promoting intercommunal hatred and antagonisms, all in the name of party politics. We must remember that if, like in 1967, when the chips are down, it is only the common man that will bear the brunt of our vaulting ambition. If ever there is a repeat of the last civil war, let no one, however highly placed, ever think that he will escape from the consequences.

I tremble with trepidation at the current campaign of ethnicity and tribalism that is sweeping through the entire length and breadth of Nigeria. I am disturbed at the campaign of calumny and denigration against some of the institutions enshrined in our Constitution. One of the greatest tragedies of our time is the conviction which inclines us towards feeling that we are right and all other people are wrong. The late Dr. Henry Ironside put the matter succinctly when he said: 'Beware lest we mistake our prejudices for our conviction.'

Mr. President, Sir, we must allow the three arms of government to perform fairly and freely and without any let, hindrance or intimidation.

Mr. President, we all appreciate the role of the press as an institution under the Constitution. The press under our Constitution shall be free to uphold the fundamental objectives and to uphold the responsibility and accountability of the government to the people. I am a passionate believer in the freedom of the press. I do sincerely believe the press should publish and be damned. Truth is, however, sacred and a press that peddles falsehood constitutes an instrument of instability.

A press that writes with a pen of poison and a tone of venom destroys its credibility as an instrument of accountability and stability. I am still convinced, Mr. President, that the Nigerian press as a veritable watchdog and as vehicle for peace and progress will not abdicate the responsibilities bestowed on it by the Constitution of the Federal Republic of Nigeria in order to pander to the whims and caprices of the political adventurers and opportunists.

Mr. President, let me end this address on a note of exhortation. Fifteen months after a return to civilian administration we are still groping in the dark. The government seems to be uncertain of its goals and confused about its purposes. Like ex-President Carter of the United States of America, President Shehu Shagari seems to be more concerned with a naturally endowed golden voice and the amiable disposition of a smooth performer. He seems to be more concerned with the appearances of doing well than with the actual quality of the work done. If he must succeed in order to achieve for himself a place of honour in the annals of our history, he must now take a more crucial look at his multitude of advisers and his so called 'friends,' as well as the palace singers and jesters who now surround him in the selfish pursuit for political patronage and spoils of office. Indeed, the President must be prepared to cross new frontiers. He must now speak for those who have no voice. He must remember those who are forgotten and must respond to the frustration of the unfortunate Nigerians to whom a cup of rice has now become a luxury. He must fulfill the aspirations of the common man whose hopes of one God, one country, and one destiny have been dashed.

Mr. President, Sir, may I end this address by thinking aloud with Shakespeare: 'There is a tide in the affairs of men, which, taken at the flood, leads on to fortune; omitted, all the voyage of their life is bound in shallows and miseries. On such a full sea are we now afloat; and we must take the current when it serves or lose our ventures.' Mr. President, Sir, the choice before President Shehu Shagari is very clear and the question before him is clearly unambiguous. 'To be or not to be, that is the question.' "

Advocacy for Minimum Wage

The statement reproduced below was made on June 3, 1981 and shows Senator Fasanmi's concern for Nigerian workers. He restated his arguments made in Parliament in 1965 during his contribution to the Appropriation Bill. His advocacy of a minimum wage indicated his passion for egalitarian and socialist society. He also called on the Federal Government to provide free education and free medical services for Nigerians as the UPN did in the States under its control. He predicted that the progressives would unite one day. The speech follows:

"Mr. President, Sir, some arguments have been canvassed particularly from some parts of the country having regard to a particular section of the Constitution which says that the National Assembly can legislate for a part of the country in fixing a minimum wage.

Mr. President, Sir, we have carried out some exercises in the Senate in regard to the question of minimum wage, and some Governors did come to the Senate to testify.

Mr. President, Sir, if one looks at Section 151 of the Constitution, it says: The Federation may make grants to a State to supplement the revenue of that State in such sum and subject to such terms and conditions as may be prescribed by the National Assembly.

This only goes to say that if the Senate does decide to pay a minimum salary, then it will not be any problem at all that the Federal Government should be able to do it through the National Assembly. They are obliged to do it. The argument that has been advanced, both in this Senate and outside, is that if you increase salaries, it will lead to inflation. The second argument that has been canvassed is that the economy of the country cannot accommodate any increase. Another argument is that the workers are not productive. They are talking of low productivity. This is certainly not fair at all. If there is a group of people that is not productive, we should look for such people not in the working class but outside the working class.

Mr. President, the argument has always been advanced that increasing salaries above the present level will lead to retrenchment and sack. I do not believe in this. And there is also the argument that the workers do need some fringe benefits. They need decent houses and very cheap food. Those who have based their policies on shelter and food have not been able to do anything. The houses that are now being built are only good for people who are living in the lepers' colonies.

As of now, after spending 18 months in office, how much have we done in order to contribute to the welfare of the workers? In terms of housing or shelter and food, what have we really done? I have no doubt in my mind that the Federal Government is in a position to organise a programme of free education for the whole country. The resources are there. I have no doubt also that they can organise a programme of free medical services but we seem to get our priorities wrong in this country. We invest our money on prestigious projects that mean nothing to the ordinary man. Nobody is saying that we should not go to Abuja, but if we look at the contracts that are being awarded at Abuja, one will have the impression that there is more than enough money to fund free education and free medical services for the people of this country.

When we have been able to do this for the workers, then we must have done something to alleviate their sufferings. Except the Government is prepared to do this, even when we talk of the minimum wage, we would not go far. So, my plea to the Government is that they should think seriously. If a government is doing very well, it is not a sin to copy it. We, on our own resources, have been able to fund free medical services and free education and these programmes are going on very well. I do not see any reason whatsoever why a Government that is alive to its responsibilities cannot do this.

As I have said earlier, the arguments that are being proffered is that an increase will lead to unprecedented inflation using Udoji as an example. The Udoji's recommendation was not well handled. I am sure that if it was well handled, it would not have led to inflation. Secondly, there is the argument that such an increase will lead to massive retrenchment and closure of factories. That is a capitalist way of argument. Another argument that is being proffered is that such a minimum wage will be justified only if the average worker is prepared to match the increase with productivity. The average worker can only improve on productivity if he has enough salary to live a decent life. You cannot isolate productivity from the type of salary which a worker gets. If you do not pay the worker enough salary, how do you want him to produce?

Mr. President, I have no doubt in my mind that the problems which we have in this country are based on: (1) the fact that we have not got our priorities right; (2) lack of dedication among the leaders; and (3) the fact that we have not got a programme and where we have a programme, we do not even follow our programme. We reduce the programme to a mere slogan. One very good thing is that once again, the progressive elements in this country will come together—and very soon too. I hope the time will come when the progressive elements in this country will come together under the banner and that day will be the day of glory for the working class of this country."

Appeal for Establishment of Industries in old Ondo State

In the quest for development of Ondo State, Senator Fasanmi co-sponsored a motion for the establishment of industries in the then Ondo State of which Ekiti State was a part. The motion was moved on July 7, 1981. His argument was based on the neglect of the State which, despite its financial contributions to the Federation through cocoa production and export, did not have major industries, unlike some states which had several major industries. The statement thus shows his concern for his constituency:

"When I said that the Federal Government has not participated as it should in the establishment of industrial enterprises in Ondo State, it is putting the matter very mildly. The truth of the matter, the whole truth and nothing but the truth, is that Ondo State, in terms of industries, has been completely neglected. Apart, perhaps, from Nigerian Romanian Wood Industries in Ondo, in which the Federal Government has what can be called a grudgingly token share, and the Oil Palm Mills in Okitipupa, over which I understand as at the moment the Federal Government is currently holding consultations with the State Government. Ondo State, with its vast mineral and forest resources, cannot boast of any single worthwhile industrial enterprise which enjoys direct Federal Government participation.

In an attempt to elucidate further on what we regard as an act of injustice that is being meted out to Ondo State, I would like to mention very briefly the situation as it obtains in most of the other States. In Kaduna State, for instance, we have the Defence Industries, we have the Peugeot Automobile Industry, which is a joint venture between the Government and some bodies, we also have the Petroleum Refinery. Coming down to Bauchi State, we have the... (*Interruptions*). We also have the Ashaka Cement Company Limited. I think this is the pattern all over. I am saying this, not with a view to saying that the Government has been partial in doing things to the other States, but my contention is that what is good for these States is also good for Ondo State.

The population of Ondo State is about three million made up of virile and industrious men and women who are determined to ensure the economic progress of the State.

Mr. President, in order to satisfy the economic yearnings and aspirations of the people, the Ondo State Government, in spite of its limited financial resources, has within a short span embarked upon a number of industrial projects but money, however, is a very big constraint.

As I mentioned in the motion, Ondo State is endowed with abundant natural resources. These are minerals like petroleum, limestone, clay, kaolin, bitumen, iron ore, marble, coal and columbite, to mention a few. The State is also rich in palm oil, palm kernel, timber, coffee, and cotton. When petroleum was not known to the economic life of Nigeria, cocoa was the mainstay of the economy of the Nation. It has to be noted, Mr. President, that Ondo State produces about 70 percent of the cocoa crop in the whole country and by way of revenue the Cocoa Board generated a surplus of over 350 million naira in 1979, which is more than the allocation of 113 million naira made by the Federal Government to Ondo State in 1980. It is indeed very sad, Mr. President, for a State that sustained the economy of the Nation in its hour of dire need should be so neglected by the Federal Government in terms of industrial development. A critical examination of the estimates of 1980 and 1981 shows very clearly the apparent neglect to which Ondo State has been subjected. When provisions were made for industries in some other States for such industries as sugar estates and factories, fish trawling and distribution, pulpwood plantation project, pulp and paper industry, commercial vehicle assembly, manufacture of clay bricks, establishment of new cement industries, integrated dairy projects, nothing practical was earmarked for Ondo State in spite of its potentialities.

Mr. President, the Ondo State Government has launched a very ambitious Fourth National Development Plan which needs the encouragement of the Federal Government. There are projects like ceramic, sheet glass, pharmaceutical, cocoa processing, brewing, cement, bitumen, *et cetera*. These projects need the encouragement of the Federal Government, if the Federal Government is to play its leadership role.

In the 1981 Approval Estimates, there is an amount of 10 million naira earmarked for industrial development centres in all states. I have no doubt, Mr. President, that Ondo State will claim a pride of place in the location of these centres.

Distinguished Senators will be shocked to hear that Ekiti, for instance, in spite of its population and vastness has not one single industry. This injustice is a contravention of the social objectives enshrined in our Constitution under fundamental objectives and directive principles of state policy. The earlier, therefore, development centres are opened in Ondo State as a matter of priority the better, because it is when there are even social, economic and political developments all over the country and all over the States that we can truly promote peace, progress and stability of Nigeria.

My colleagues and I who come from Ondo State feel terribly sad at the neglect in the industrial development in Ondo State and failure of the Federal Government to come to our aid. We are, however, not bitter about our plight and I am sure that this distinguished Senate known for its sense of justice and fair play will give its overwhelming support to this motion.

We have come to the aid of educationally backward and disadvantaged areas of this country because of our commitment to the policy of even development. I have no doubt in my mind that my colleagues will give the same support to our request that the Federal Government should give priority attention to the establishment of economically viable industrial enterprises in Ondo State through direct government participation."

Criteria for State Creation and Advocacy for Ekiti and Osun States

Senator Fasanmi's statement on the Procedure Bill for the creation of States started with caution especially, as regards the issue of the proliferation of States. He, therefore, called for a joint Senate-House Committee to streamline the procedure.

Senator Fasanmi also called for the creation of Ekiti and Osun States. The statement was made on June 8, 1982. Osun and Ekiti States were finally created in 1991 and 1996 respectively.

The Senator's statement:

"When the Bill before us was first laid, many Senators wanted to know whether the Bill was a Private Members' Bill or a Government Bill. However, it is now very clear, judging from the proceedings in the House of Representatives yesterday, that the Bill before us is an Executive Bill arising from the deliberations of seventeen wise men. That being the case, Mr. President, if we are genuinely interested in the creation of more States in Nigeria in the life of the present administration, certain constitutional issues must be resolved with speed and dispatch.

Mr. President, I must observe that if the stability of the Nation must be preserved, then something has to be done to keep in check the proliferation of States. While a case could be made for genuine demands, every attempt must also be made to arrest frivolous agitations. I am sure that if the twenty governments of the Federation keep scrupulously to the Fundamental Objectives and Directive Principles of State Policy enshrined in Chapter II of our Constitution, if the gap between the urban and rural areas is bridged by a meaningful programme of development, the demand for more States will be minimised. However, it is my candid opinion that after the current exercise, a new provision should be built into the Constitution to regulate further the creation of new States, so that no new State could be created at any interval less than twenty years.

For now, however, I wish to say that there is a need for greater cooperation and better understanding between the Senate and the House of Representatives Committee in regulating the procedure for the creation of new States and for matters connected therewith. There have been for some time now, intensive activities on the part of our colleagues of the House of Representatives Committee on the modalities for the creation of new States. Some of these activities appear to me to border more on the sensational and less on the fundamental and the real. Each arm of the National Assembly is free to conduct its affairs and regulate its procedure in the manner it thinks fit and appropriate where the agitation for the creation of new States has been well articulated. In order, however, to ensure that the legitimate aspirations of our people are met, both the Senate Committee and House of Representatives Committee on the creation of new States should fuse into one body so as to avoid needless duplication of efforts and unnecessary dissipation of energy on purely procedural matters.

Mr. President, Sir, may I end my brief contribution to this debate by saying again that with me and my colleagues on this side of the Senate, the creation of new States is an article of faith. It is on record that I led a delegation of prominent leaders of Ekiti to present a request both to the President of the Senate and the Clerk of the House of Representatives for the creation of an Ekiti State.

Furthermore, I have lived in Osogbo in Osun Division for the past thirty-one years. I make bold to say that nowhere perhaps is the agitation for a new State so articulated as in Osun Division. Both the people of Ekiti, my hometown, and Osun Division, my domicile town, in particular as well as other communities who are genuinely seeking for new States are critically watching our deliberations. It will be very uncharitable to play politics with their genuine demand and aspirations. On our part, we are prepared to consider this Bill dispassionately and having regards to our oath of office, we shall ensure that all legal hurdles are constitutionally dismantled so that all those who want new States created can realise the fulfilment of their objectives in the life of the present administration."

Comment on "The Economic Stabilisation (Temporary Provisions) Order" on June 22, 1982

The economic recession in Nigeria between 1981-1983 attracted some cogent comments by Senator Fasanmi. He critically examined the measures taken by President Shagari to stabilize the economy. The suggestions made by the Senator included a need for broader briefing of the Senate and the private sector. In addition, he advised the Government to elicit views from the private sector as well as the populace on the impact of the measures imposed by the Shagari Government.

Senator Fasanmi stated as follows:

"Mr. President, Sir, at a special joint session of the National Assembly on 19th April, 1982, the President of the Federal Republic of Nigeria briefed members of the National Assembly on the precarious state of our national economy.

At the meeting, the President indicated his intention to take remedial measures in order to revamp the economy. In view of the seriousness of the problem, the National Assembly gave the President the powers which he sought under the Economic Stabilisation (Temporary Provisions) Act, 1982 which we are discussing today. It is needless crying over spilt milk. The powers which the President sought from the National Assembly were virtually given to him on a platter of gold.

As contained in the Official Gazette of the 20th April, 1982, the President has introduced far reaching changes under the Act in respect of customs duties, excise duties, import prohibition as well as export prohibition. Judging from public reactions, there is no doubt that these changes have been biting very hard. Since, however, there is a need for sacrifices by all sectors to make "Nigeria great," Nigerians should regard some of the present austerity measures as the price they have to pay in order to make Nigeria self-reliant.

The Economic Stabilisation (Temporary Provisions) Act 1982 shall cease to have effect at the expiration of a period of 12 months from the date upon which it came into operation.

Mr. President, in spite of this provision in the Bill, I think there is a need for an occasional review of the Act or, in the alternative, the National Assembly deserves to have a quarterly progress report of the measures taken. I remember that when the President brought the Bill, some of the Senators raised this point and said it was very necessary either quarterly or every six months that the Senate should be briefed. But that amendment was defeated. However, Mr. President, I still feel that it is in the interest of the nation that this has to be done. It is not enough for the Minister of Finance to tell the nation on the pages of newspapers, or any other news media, that some substantial progress has been recorded without quantifying such progress.

Mr. President, Sir, we would like to know what benefits have accrued to the Nation as a result of the measures taken. I am aware that we are discussing the Economic Stabilisation (Temporary Provisions) Orders of 1982. We are not discussing economic destabilisation. I am talking against things that could destabilise the economy. We need to look critically at some of the provisions of this Bill. We need also to consider the biting effects the Bill has had on the people of this country. I, therefore, completely buy the suggestion made by a distinguished Senator that it may be necessary for us to meet all sections of our community, particularly the business community, to find out exactly what they feel about this Bill.

This is the point I want to touch on. This is why I think we should have an in-depth study of the Bill we are now considering. With my short but non-controversial contribution, I humbly suggest that, at the appropriate time, we should, after discussing this Bill at length, invite, not the Senate Committee on Commerce at this time, but the whole Senate, the business community, to find out exactly the effects it will have on the populace.

The Senate Leader talked about cars and cubic capacities. Some of us are not talking about such things. We want the people of this country to be able to have two decent square meals a day. It is very difficult to make ends meet in this country. A country that cannot provide for its teeming population and suffering masses definitely cannot do anything when there is an uprising.

I am becoming increasingly apprehensive about the future of this country. If anything will spark off trouble in this country, it is the economy and how it has been mismanaged by some people. The only solution is that everybody is anxiously looking forward to 1983. We, on this side of the Senate, do not want to do anything that would disturb the peaceful handing over of the reins of the government to progressive elements in 1983."

CHAPTER THREE

STATEMENTS TO ALL PROGRESSIVES CONGRESS AND EGBE AFENIFERE

Senator Fasanmi's contributions reproduced in this chapter are concerned with his suggestions and advice which were largely made before and after the 2015 elections; an epochal period in the history of Nigeria when the opposition party, APC, defeated the ruling party, PDP. The first time ever, an opposition party came to power in Nigeria.

These statements cover a variety of policy matters and issues; they demonstrate the Senator's deep interest in public policies that will ensure the security and welfare of the people.

Only a few of these statements have been selected for publication in this book.

Towards Free and Fair Elections in 2015 (January, 2015)

Free and fair elections that are held regularly are one of the ways through which democracies legitimise governments. Through elections in which citizens express themselves without intimidation or bribery and where the vote of each citizen counts, peaceful change of government is made possible. However, the history of plebiscitary democracy in Nigeria is checkered.

From 1959 till 2011, there have been nine federal elections, two held under parliamentary system of government while the rest were conducted under the presidential system introduced in 1979. Three of the nine elections were supervised by departing praetorian regimes (1979, 1993 and 1999) while the remaining six were conducted by civilian governments. Except for the 1993 presidential election, which was deliberately undermined by the self-styled military president, elections held under military oversight were generally better, even though they were far from perfect.

Incumbent civilian governments have generally used their incumbency to their advantage during elections. Among other things, incumbents have used the national treasury as their party purse whilst also collecting bribes from their appointees and contractors to fund their campaigns. State media, radio and television, have been used as the publicity arm of the ruling party.

In addition, officials in the office of the current incumbent who are paid out of Nigerian treasury are a mouthpiece of the ruling party. These men and women whose employment depended on being a megaphone of the PDP and aggressive defender of the incumbent owe their loyalty not to the people of Nigeria but to the incumbent. In the American political system where Nigeria borrowed the form of government, if not the spirit of its constitution, this is not the case. The cantankerous, inciting, and abusive statements of the supporters of the incumbent President are sufficient, in a mature democracy, to cost him the election. Indeed, a case of gross electoral malfeasance in 1972 orchestrated from the American White House led to the resignation of President Richard Nixon in 1974.

In Nigeria, incumbents or their party agents especially senior apparatchik of the current administration are mounting undue pressure on the chief electoral officer to ensure re-election of the incumbent. Regrettably, a tragic drama is currently playing out in which there are speculations that the chief electoral officer, who is not a civil servant, may be asked to proceed on so-called terminal leave. The import of such a sinister plan is to replace the electoral officer with someone that will be amenable to the plan of the ruling party to swing the election in favour of the PDP presidential candidate.

If I may digress, were such a plan to change the chief electoral officer implemented, it will not only taint the presidential election but mar the reputation of Nigeria thus eroding its quest as a democratic state. Nigerians need to be reminded that the chief electoral officer being hounded by agents of the incumbent was the one who presided over Dr. Jonathan's election in 2011.

From my reading of sections 154 (1,3),155 (1) and 157 (I,2) of the 1999 Constitution regarding certain Federal Executive Bodies, the President has to follow the procedure for appointment and removal of the Chairman of the Independent National Electoral Commission. From the composition of the Senate, the President is not likely to muster the two-thirds (about 73 Senators) required for his removal. The plan to remove Professor Jega through illegal terminal leave, if true, will precipitate political and constitutional crises that might have far reaching consequences for the polity.

Apart from efforts to compromise the chief electoral umpire, incumbents have also used the state security apparatus as gendarmes of the ruling party tactically deploying them to intimidate supporters of the opposition, curbing the freedom of opposition to campaign, and providing cover for blatant rigging. With less than three weeks to the presidential election, questions about permanent voter card readers are being raised by the PDP. This is yet another ruse to scuttle the election.

The antics of the PDP in 2015 is turning out to be a gross repeat of the 2003 and the 2007 elections. Both elections were marred by ruling party violence and unabashed rigging. Human Rights Watch described the 2003 elections as not credible, and the 2007 elections as deeply flawed. The British government in its statement on the 2007 elections wrote that the elections fell "short of the standards for credible, free and fair elections and the worst in Nigeria's post-independence electoral history." Given these developments, I have deep apprehensions about the 2015 elections. I am equally fearful for my beloved country, a country where I was privileged to serve as a member of the Federal Parliament in 1964 and as a Senator in 1979.

How can we ensure a level playing field for all parties and how can we avoid the abyss? First, is for the incumbent to commit to and demonstrate fairness. The President should demonstrate leadership by fostering an atmosphere of amity and sportsmanship by putting a leash on the attack dogs in the PDP and by total and complete transparency in election procedures. Second, security agencies should not only be independent but should be seen to be so by all Nigerians. The independence of electoral officials should be respected and guaranteed. Third, respected non-partisan national leaders from all six geopolitical zones should appeal to contestants to allow free and fair elections.

The National Assembly in the exercise of its oversight powers should immediately hold legislative hearings in which heads of security agencies (Police, Department of State Security, Chief of Defense Staff, National Security Adviser) should reaffirm their neutrality during the elections and pledge their allegiance to the Constitution of the Federal Republic of Nigeria rather than to any party or candidate.

To further ensure fairness of the elections, the United Nations Electoral Assistance Division should urgently be invited to assist in the 2015 elections. In addition, the UN and Commonwealth should send electoral observers to watch the conduct of the presidential and gubernatorial elections. Their presence might constrain electoral manipulations and discourage the old pattern of election rigging.

Some Nigerians might argue that Nigeria's sovereignty will be undermined by UN and Commonwealth involvement in the elections. There are two responses to this line of thinking. First, there is no absolute sovereignty. Our interdependent world has eroded the notion of unfettered sovereignty. Second, since 1991, over 100 countries have requested and benefitted from UN electoral assistance. Among the beneficiaries are Brazil, Indonesia, Bangladesh, and South Africa. Even Nigeria, under the United Nations Development Programme (UNDP), was a beneficiary of UN's electoral assistance in 1999. During the 1999 elections, UNDP contributed 200,000 dollars while Japan, Canada, and the European Union donated several million dollars to the exercise. In effect, the United Nations and donors made inputs through financial assistance to the election process. What is required now is for more visible presence by the UN, the Commonwealth and civil society organisations to ensure that the elections scheduled for March 28 and April 11, 2015, are held in an atmosphere unencumbered by ruling party manipulations.

UN electoral assistance is urgently needed to ensure the integrity of the forthcoming elections.

Suggested themes for APC Presidential Candidate (February 2015)

Introduction

Nigeria is at a major crossroad. The upcoming March 28 elections provide Nigerians with the opportunity to choose between progress and light or darkness and backwardness. The All Progressives Congress represents light and advancement while the other party is the party of corruption and darkness.

The symbol of the APC, broom, is meant to sweep away the 'Peoples Deception Party'. A party which in the last sixteen years has eaten Nigeria to its bones. A party that has brought ill luck to Nigeria. A party which is drenched in corruption, deception and incompetence.

Nigerians face numerous difficulties daily and the PDP

appears unconcerned; it caters to only the rich, privileged and well connected. I shall enumerate some of the problems facing all Nigerians which the PDP has either ignored or it has not handled well.

Security

The foremost issue confronting Nigeria is security. No Nigerian is safe anywhere. Nigerians are killed daily by Boko Haram, armed robbers, kidnappers, ritual murderers, and murderous drivers on our highways. According to Nigeria Stability and Reconciliation Programme, a British research group, about 60,558 Nigerians died due to violence between 2006 and 2014. Add to this the killing by the nihilistic Boko Haram which murdered 2,000 Nigerians and razed the Baga community of Borno State to the ground. Another independent research body, the well-known Mo Ibrahim Foundation, ranked Nigeria poorly in safety and rule of law.

The response of the PDP Administration to the crime against Nigerians is to deny the number of those killed in Baga; rather it was more concerned with the regrettable death of French journalists at the hand of deranged men. The reaction of the Administration follows the previous pattern which is to ignore or downplay the crimes against Nigerians.

The unchecked violence of Boko Haram and other conflicts in Nigeria has displaced about 3.3 million Nigerians, almost 2 percent of our population. We therefore have the unenviable record of having the highest number of refugees in Africa.

In their fifteen years of governing Nigeria, the PDP, despite spending over five billion dollars on security in the 2014 budget, has not provided security for Nigerians. It is time to change the President that has failed to secure Nigeria.

Nigerians should elect Buhari, a man who understands security issues. He will end the state of insecurity and the siege on Nigeria.

The APC solution to insecurity will be dual. It will deal with security as well as socioeconomic issues that cause insecurity. Briefly, the military will be well equipped, disciplined and provided with incentives to confront and defeat Boko Haram. Equally, communities will be engaged in policing their communities.

Regarding socioeconomic issues, we shall provide a master-plan to develop the Northeast and areas affected by violence. In addition, there will be programmes to provide employment, de-radicalize our youths, and promote religious moderation and tolerance.

Economy

Nigeria is the largest economy in Africa with a Gross Domestic Product of 510 billion dollars, yet 60 percent of Nigerians live in poverty. A reason for the poverty is corruption and mismanagement. According to Afrobarometer, a well-respected research organisation, 81 percent of Nigerians surveyed said that management of the economy under PDP is poor. Nigeria has lost trillions of naira due to corruption. The looters go unpunished under PDP watch. For instance, some PDP former Ministers and Governors indicted by the Economic and Financial Crimes Commission (EFCC) for corruption are campaign managers and advisors of the party. Nigerians should ask what has happened to the EFCC trial of all these people. Not one high political official under the PDP Administration has been convicted of corruption; hence the PDP campaign pledge to fight corruption is a promise which, like those made in 2011, will not be fulfilled.

Another source of financial leakage is import waivers. The waivers cost the economy billions of naira. For instance, an engineering company granted an import waiver turned around to use it to import rice. A former PDP Governor who was issued a 500 million naira import license to import vehicles for his state for a cultural festival turned around to sell the license to a motor vehicle dealer.

Research done by Nigeria Politico listed some of the beneficiaries of import waivers. The list is made up of politically connected Nigerians including PDP bigwigs and businessmen from two Asian countries. These are the ones who donated 21 billion naira to the PDP campaign chest. There is no doubt that the donation is a bribe to the PDP so that the donors could continue to rob Nigerians. According to Nigeria Customs Service, Nigeria lost 1.4 trillion naira to import waivers. This is money that could have been used to repair refineries, upgrade and maintain infrastructure, create employment, and pay salaries to government workers.

The PDP must therefore be voted out of office for Nigeria to make progress under APC. We urge Nigerians to use their vote to bring APC to power.

Buhari as President will ensure that anti-corruption agencies such as EFCC and Independent Corrupt Practices Commission (ICPC) are enabled to do their work. Under APC, those who engage in corruption will face the full weight of the law.

An APC government will also work to reduce unemployment through creation of a public works administration that will hire Nigerians to work in the repair and construction of infrastructure projects. We shall also train youths to make them employable. We shall also promote entrepreneurship.

The APC government will promote an environment to encourage investment flow into Nigeria. The taxation system will be revised to streamline multiple taxations. States will be allowed to have more revenue at their disposal.

Electricity

On January 3, 2011, Dr. Jonathan declared 'If I am voted into power, within the next four years (2015), the issue of power will become a thing of the past...' adding that 'If I cannot improve on power within the period, it means I can do nothing.' Of course, till date, Nigeria is still essentially a land of literal darkness in the night despite expenditure of over 50 billion dollars on power. Nigerians spend about 80 billion naira annually to buy and fuel their generators. The privatization of power has not led to the promised improvement in power as the companies that bought the transmission lines neither have the capacity nor the capital to run the power lines. Whilst we do not intend to reverse the privatization already done, we shall ensure that the interest of the Nigerian public is protected. We shall also encourage investment in other power sources especially renewable energy such as solar, wind and thermal energy.

Petroleum and the Nigerian Economy

We all know that the mainstay of the Nigerian economy is oil, which generates over 90 percent of our foreign exchange. We are all practically dependent on oil and the industry has made us very lazy, suffering as we are, from what economists call resource-curse. Oil, while benefiting us, has also led to massive corruption and violence in oil-producing areas. Yet, while we produce crude oil, we import refined oil products while our refineries are either idle or under produce refined petroleum.

The APC will ensure that the problems of the oil industry are resolved and that Nigerians on whose land drilling takes place are well compensated. We shall also ensure that the Nigerian National Petroleum Company follows the best global practice.

Agriculture

Agriculture is very important to us all. It provides our food and it is a major contributor to our gross domestic product, contributing about 41 percent. It also employs about 70 percent of our population.

Problems of Nigerian agriculture are several. They include soil erosion, post-harvest loss, food importation and insufficient investment in the sector. The Jonathan Administration has been telling us of the so-called progress in agriculture such as increased food production. Nigerians have yet to feel this increase as they still buy rice imported from Asia at inflated prices. We can and should produce enough rice to feed ourselves.

Our solution to our agricultural problems will include incentives to farmers to produce more food including rice. We will work with farmers to reduce post-harvest loss, provide and ensure that fertilisers reach the end users and not middlemen who become rich by hijacking and selling the fertilisers at inflated prices. We shall also deal with the problem of soil erosion and encourage states to place priority on agriculture as part of an aggressive policy of the federal government to increase food production. We shall also diversify our economy so that agriculture and industries related to it will thrive.

We urge all Nigerians to turn out on February 14 and 28 to vote out the PDP whose rule is ruining Nigeria.

Reflections on February 2015

As February 2015 draws near, global focus is on Nigeria. There are several reasons for this attention. There is no doubt, that the first reason for the attention is that elections are to be held in the most populous country in Africa, thus bringing into bold relief, the march or otherwise of plebiscitary democracy in an important African country.

A second and definitely compelling reason for preoccupation with the elections is that the elections of 14th and 28th of February are scheduled to be held in a situation in which the nihilistic insurgent group, Boko Haram, is said to control about twenty percent of Nigerian land mass. The seizure of Nigerian territory by Boko Haram has resulted in the displacement of over 600,000 Nigerians and made another 80,000 to seek refuge in Cameroon and Chad. In effect, thousands of these Nigerians may not be able to exercise their right to vote.

Yet, a third factor why the election has attracted the attention of the international community is the unpleasant history of electoral malfeasance in Nigeria. Past elections in Nigeria are characterised by rigging, switching of election results, vote suppression, and use of public media to promote the governing party. In addition, security forces are deployed by the federal government to intimidate the opposition, their candidates and supporters. The inexplicable gubernatorial election result of June 21, 2014 in Ekiti is still fresh.

Regrettably, we appear not to have learnt from past gross electoral chicanery of 1964, 1965, and 1983 when turmoil followed elections of those years. Indeed, the pattern of past electoral malpractices appears to have reared its head again or is in the offing as seen in recent events. Briefly, these events are purchase of voter cards, character assassinations, disruptive court cases, false opinion surveys, and sudden transfer of top police officials. In addition, the PDP-led federal government is said to have released billions of naira to farmers, in order to influence Nigerian voters.

Instead of investing in infrastructure, the PDP, on the eve of a crucial election, is bribing Nigerians with a one-time so-called "stomach infrastructure." After the elections, the PDP will abandon ordinary Nigerians to darkness, hunger, starvation, and unemployment whilst PDP political barons feed fat in the house of patronage and continue their looting of Nigerian treasury. This, at a time when sixty percent of Nigerians live below the global poverty level which is less than 175 naira a day.

In the history of independent Nigeria, not once has there been change of power at the federal level between the ruling party and opposition. African countries such as the Republic of Benin, Ghana, Senegal and Mauritius have peacefully voted out ruling parties in favour of the opposition. Indeed, power has changed hands between government and opposition twice in Ghana, Republic of Benin, and Mauritius. These African states thus meet the test of Professor Samuel Huntington, late American political scientist, as democratic states. Nigerians can advance and deepen democracy by peacefully voting out PDP and installing APC in power.

The elections coming up this month thus provide Nigerians the opportunity to make history by putting in power the opposition APC which will work for Nigerians, a party that will not loot the treasury, and a party that will truly serve the Nigerian people and bring genuine change.

When Nigerians effect peaceful change through the ballot, the country can then begin the arduous task of building institutions of state that will provide security for all, improve the economy for the benefit of all Nigerians, and hold all public officials accountable.

Statement to the Leaders of All Progressives Congress (April 2015)

Dear Leaders of All Progressives Congress,

I congratulate all members of our party warmly on the historic achievement of our party in the March 28, 2015 elections. The election of President Muhammadu Buhari as President of the Federal Republic and control of the Federal Legislative Houses effective May 29, 2015 represent a paradigm shift in the politics of Nigeria.

For close to six decades, progressives have sought the

mandate to govern Nigeria but have not succeeded until now. The great and sustained efforts deployed by the leaders of our party throughout the Federation contributed to the success of this outstanding achievement. I salute and commend you all and also thank you for allowing me to witness in my lifetime a progressive government in control of the Nigerian Federation.

We, in the progressive party, know that there is still more work ahead as APC begins the arduous task of reconstructing a new Nigeria that is safe and secure; a new Nigeria that is free of corruption; a new Nigeria where citizens are gainfully employed, and a Nigeria whose government is truly serving the people.

I wish all our party leaders success in the implementation of our party programmes.

Long live APC

Long live the Federal Republic of Nigeria.

Managing APC Success (April 2015)

APC success in the 2015 elections was achieved through unceasing efforts of Nigerians from different states, regions, faiths and socioeconomic backgrounds working together as a team to work for change. The victory achieved at the polls is a seismic shift in Nigerian politics and brings with it the opportunity to reshape Nigeria into an effective, progressive and leading African state and a respectable member of the international community.

No doubt, the most important prerequisite for managing Nigeria creditably is to manage ourselves very well. We must be disciplined, stay united, focused, shun conspicuous consumption, and be accountable to the electorate. Further, we must work hard and serve Nigerians with all our strengths and not oppress them with our power. When differences arise in our ranks, we should manage them through reconciliation not with hard line positions that will deepen the differences and allow our opponents to take advantage of the differences to factionalise the APC and undermine our unity. Useful lessons should be learned from the implosion of the PDP which practically self-destructed. Hence, a Reconciliation Committee made up of elders in the APC that have reputation for fairness should be established at all levels of governance to manage conflicts.

As part of our managing APC for successful governance, we must be fair to all sections of the country. Progress, equity, discipline, and fairness to all should be our guiding principles.

Once we are united and disciplined, we should create institutions that will enable us to govern well to meet the aspirations of Nigerians.

A great gap in governance in Nigeria is the absence of research institutions to undertake research for political parties on public policy issues such as security, economy, education, power, and intergovernmental relations. APC should establish a research group that will serve as its think tank to plan strategies for the achievement of party agenda. Each state should be encouraged to have its own think tank. Data and analysis collected at the state level should be shared with the main APC research team.

APC research organisation should also be responsible for monitoring APC programmes to identify what works, lessons learned and how to apply these lessons to other programmes and governance issues. In addition, the research group should periodically conduct scientific opinion surveys on the performance of the party and impact of APC policies. Through the proposed research group, APC will be entrenching problem solving tactics in Nigeria.

If a decision is made to establish the research group, its first task should be the compression of party manifesto into an actionable programme for information and use by all APC governments at state and federal levels. The use of such a programme by all APC states, taking into account the peculiarities of each state, will create coherence in all APC governed states. This will be a significant step in achieving sustainable development.

Of course, there are publicly funded research institutions that conduct research into social, economic and political issues but the civil service does not generally utilise such research findings to guide public policy. Further, there is always a time lag between the conduct of research and the output of research for use by decision-makers. APC research group will therefore serve as a forum which the party could use in lieu of weak or non-performance of publicly funded research institutions.

Another step in managing APC success is to develop an APC federal legislative agenda based on the manifesto of the party. APC legislators and the President should meet to prioritise legislations that will address the numerous problems of Nigeria. APC legislators in the National Assembly should be disciplined and ensure that, as the majority party, they elect one of their own as President and Speaker of the Senate and House of Representatives respectively. Failure to elect credible APC members into these pivotal legislative posts will derail the APC agenda and undermine the effectiveness of the party.

A major outcry against the outgoing PDP President and the National Assembly under the control of his party is the high cost of governance in Nigeria. APC legislators should upon being sworn into office visit the issue with a view to streamlining the cost of governance.

Yet, another issue in managing APC success is to show restraint to provocations by the PDP. While the statement of APC could be strong, those from the Presidency should be measured and mature.

Finally, APC at all times should be democratic in its procedures and processes; it should endear itself to Nigerians by governing responsibly, and it should respect the rights of all citizens through upholding the rule of law and the constitution. Through responsive and responsible governance, the party could ensure itself of a long stay in power.

The Imperative for Sustainable Change: A few Ideas for the President-elect and APC Leadership (April 2015)

The campaign theme of the All Progressives Congress (APC) in the last Presidential election was "change". In figurative and practical terms, the "change" advocated by the APC is not only change of personnel at the federal and state levels where PDP is in control, but also change in policy and style of governance. The people of Nigeria in exercising their democratic rights endorsed the call for change and placed the APC to be in control of the change.

Through the mandate given the APC to change Nigeria, it can be assumed that Nigerians expect that governance will not be business as usual; that government will be clean, effective, efficient, and at all times accountable.

It can also be safely assumed that Nigerians want sustainable change that will have positive impact on their lives as well as those of their children. Sustainable change depends on appropriate policies implemented by people with integrity and vision who will work to build institutions that will endure. APC can draw on many party members and several Nigerian technocrats who are sympathetic to the party platform. These Nigerians can transform the vision of the party into an instrument for sustainable change. Therefore, the initial step in the APC's Agenda for Change is to select men of proven integrity and a good record of service from different geopolitical regions to be part of the change team and to serve as change catalysts in Nigeria.

Nigerians expect change to be immediate and visible. Thus, quick-win projects should be seriously considered. Pilot programmes of such projects should be rolled out in each geopolitical zone soonest to enable Nigerian citizens know that the Buhari Administration is a departure from PDP past administrations.

A matter that should buy policy space for the APC administration while more difficult issues are addressed is the seventy percent duty on imported vehicles imposed by the outgoing Jonathan Administration ostensibly to fund motor car assembly plants in Nigeria. The Buhari Administration should announce its indefinite suspension whilst it is studying the impact of the policy on Nigerians particularly the middle class.

Another policy initiative is in the area of public safety and security. The Buhari Administration, while developing a comprehensive safety and security package, could immediately upon assumption of office, direct the police to establish 24-hour police patrol on all major highways of the federation. Specially equipped paramilitary men with night goggles in powerful vehicles equipped with search lights should be deployed on major roadways that are travelled at night. Night duty allowance should be given to those on night duty patrol. Their performance should be measured through reduced crime incidents. Each patrol team should be asked to keep a log book daily to record incidents which should be subjected to inspection by the Inspectorate Division of Safety and Security Bureau, a body that should be independent of the police. In the immediate future, that is any time from September 2015, the patrols should be reinforced with helicopters equipped with search lights and gunships to complement vehicle patrols. The use of drones and helicopter gunships in the North-East should be considered a matter of priority and be part of the security package for the region.

As part of the package to be launched upon his assumption of office, the President-elect should constitute a panel to establish benchmarks for parastatals and public agencies that provide service to the public. For example, the Federal Airport Authority of Nigeria should ensure that all arriving passengers at the Murtala International Airport clear immigration and customs in under 90 minutes. Telephone numbers to call for poor, inefficient, and discourteous service at international airports should be conspicuously displayed in several places in the airport. Erring officers, or a group of officers, should be sanctioned for poor performance, rudeness or soliciting bribes.

To let visitors know that there is change in Nigeria, the Murtala International Airport and its perimeter stretching from the airport to local airport in Ikeja and to the Apapa-Oshodi exchange should be secured and landscaped. The roadways to the airport should be lit every night with standby generators and patrolled 24 hours by a specially created Airport Police. The police patrol should be seen every ten minutes by citizens. The patrol team should be strictly warned to desist from corruption. Indeed, sting operations to catch corrupt elements in the patrol should be mounted periodically. What is planned for the Murtala International Airport should be done for other international airports in Kano, Abuja, and Port Harcourt.

Finally, Nigerians should be told that solutions to decades of decay will be developed gradually and implemented methodically to prevent relapse to old patterns of degeneration. In addition, the responsibility to change Nigeria rests with all Nigerians and hence Nigerians should be briefed periodically about proposed changes and requested to buy into the agenda for change. Nigerians should be called upon to support the Administration by behaving responsibly.

Introspection and Retrospection in my nine decades of existence (September 2015)

I am thankful to God for His numerous blessings on me in my nearly nine decades of existence. The Lord Almighty has blessed me with a long, healthy. and good life. I am blessed with dutiful and loving children and grandchildren as well as respectful and caring brothers and sisters. I find joy and fulfillment in all of them.

I had hoped my wife would be by my side as I mark this day, but the Lord called her a year ago to eternity. Her passing left a big void in my life, but I am still thankful to God for having her in my life for over 60 years. Today and every day, I miss her very much.

The support of my biological family has been complemented with that of my political family, especially those in the progressive movement. I pray to God the Creator and Sustainer to grant my family and political associates a long, healthy and prosperous life. May the progressive light shine and cover the whole of Nigeria.

Ladies and gentlemen, kindly permit me to use this occasion to talk about Nigeria, a country in whose politics I have been directly and indirectly involved for well over half a century. I have been privileged to witness the pre-independence struggle of Nigeria and its post-independence travails. My journey as a political participant-observer of the events in Nigeria began in the late 1940s with my presence at the campaign rallies in Lagos of Dr. Nnamdi Azikiwe whose rhetorical flourish galvanized several youths to support the demand for an independent Nigeria. I later joined the Action Group which Professor Richard Sklar, an American political scientist, described as the then best organised political party in Africa. Under the banner of the party, I was elected to the Federal Parliament in 1964. I was also privileged to serve as a Senator in the Second Republic (1979-1983) under the platform of the Unity Party of Nigeria, a born-again version of the Action Group, led by Chief Obafemi Awolowo, and I also identified with the Social Democratic Party during the transition to democracy under General Ibrahim Babangida.

In the post-1999 military era, I have been affiliated with progressive political parties from the Alliance for Democracy to the Action Congress for Nigeria and currently I am in the All Progressives Congress. My political affiliation marks me as a progressive and I have been referred to as "Baba the Progressive Activist."

As a politician who belonged to a principled opposition party in the First Republic, that is the Action Group, we bore the brunt of Federal Government repression through a policy of destabilization of Western Nigeria and elimination of the Action Group, the then ruling party in the region. The partisan intrusion of the Federal Government in the Western Region and the gross electoral malfeasance of 1964 and 1965 led to the overthrow of that Government. The truncation of democracy in January 1966 and the darkness that settled over Nigeria thereafter lasted for several decades.

When, fifty-four years ago, we exchanged the British Union Jack for the double green interlaced white Nigerian flag, we were enthusiastic and hopeful that given our large population and mineral resources, Nigeria could rapidly achieve development. The expectations of Nigerians even though misplaced then were that Nigeria would lead Africa. We were unmindful of our handicaps which consisted of a sorely unstable federation which sat on a wobbling tripod.

Without doubt, some progress has been made in certain

spheres of Nigerian life. Our population, which has historically been inflated, has more than quadrupled; from 45 million in 1960 we are now an incredulous 181 million people. Higher education institutions which were three in 1960 (Ibadan, Nsukka, and Yaba) now number about 128. Tarred roads which were few then now cover many parts of Nigeria though majority of the roads have gaping potholes. Phone communication which was enjoyed in major regional capitals and certain urban areas in 1960 is now available almost everywhere in Nigeria. Of course, we now enjoy civil rule even though chequered.

Yet, there are enduring problems and great challenges. Many of these problems are intertwined and a few go back to colonial times. In retrospect, there is still no consensus on the structure of our nominal federation. To this may be added gross mismanagement and endemic corruption in many states. Several of our states also lack good and effective leadership. The paucity of good leadership at several levels of governance has aggravated the problems facing Nigeria and made difficult the development of good and effective institutions.

Nationalist leaders in the persons of Chief Obafemi Awolowo, Dr. Nnamdi Azikiwe and Sir Ahmadu Bello were disciplined and had a high level of integrity that cannot be matched by several of our current leaders. They were not known for stealing public funds and for relishing in profligacy and ostentatious consumption as today's leaders are. The founding fathers were thrifty and competitive in bringing development to their respective regions. Some current leaders are awash with pilfered public funds, running into billions of naira, which are diverted to private use with impunity. Those who impoverished

Nigerians are celebrated and returned to office. Former public officials convicted of financial crimes in other countries where the rule of law is the norm return to Nigeria to be given clemency. Several individuals who face corruption charges are let go through political influence or have their cases adjourned endlessly by a compromised judiciary. Our elections are yet to meet acceptable global standards. Our reputation on the global index of transparency is abysmal as Transparency International, a global non-governmental organisation, which promotes accountability and integrity, placed us in number 144 out of 177 countries.

On other indices of governance, such as safety and rule of law, participation and human rights, sustainable development and human development, we scored low. These indices developed by the Mo Ibrahim Foundation placed Nigeria in the forty-first position out of 52 states in Africa. In effect, we are in the group of the bottom twenty percent. We have beaten our chest to proclaim that we are doing well, pointing out the increase in Nigeria's economic growth which the African Development Bank put at 7.4%. However, this has been a jobless growth as the level of unemployment in Nigeria as of last year was put at 37%. Youth and graduate unemployment is chronic, and has fed the raging crime wave and religious fundamentalism in Nigeria.

As indicated earlier, the ills that plague Nigeria are several and the challenges facing the country are numerous. Three decades of military misrule increased these problems. Efforts by the military to impose their vision of a unitary Nigeria through a process of socio-political engineering seemed to have failed. This is evident in the existence of insolvent states, enduring ethnic conflicts, and rise of a very virulent form of religious fundamentalism and sectarianism that engulf a certain part of the country. The violent religious fundamentalists have made it clear that their goal is to destroy secular Nigeria.

In my view, the most fundamental issue that poses existential threat to the survival of the country is structural. We need to agree to a true federal structure in which power flows from the regions to the central government, and not the current system or those proposed by a hand-picked constitutional conference. In a genuine federal system, which we practiced until praetorian intrusion in 1966, each region had its own constitution, two of the three regions had their police forces, each maintained a separate judiciary, and the revenue derivation formula was in favour of regions from where the revenue was generated.

The vast expansion of federal power has neither produced a more united Nigeria nor has it led to a developed country. Indeed, it has led to increase in centrifugal forces as several issues which were under the old regions such as sharia and local government have been brought under the central government. These local cultural issues have inflamed passion and threatened the existence of Nigeria. Those who oppose return to new regional arrangements are more interested in the patronage enjoyed by them under the current dysfunctional system.

Under a regional system, the current states will continue to exist while several responsibilities usurped by the central government will be transferred to the regions. Of course, each region will determine its political structure, bicameral or unicameral legislature, number of Ministries and maintain a police force, among other things.

Let me digress to discuss a major pitfall of the current unitary structure dressed in false federal garb. I have in mind the federal misuse of security forces especially during elections. This has been the pattern since independence. For example, the Native Authority Police were used to manipulate elections in favour of the governing party in Northern Nigeria, while the Nigeria National Democratic Party, an affiliate of the Northern People's Congress, did the same in Western Region in 1965. In 1983, the police functioned as a wing of the National Party of Nigeria arresting members of the opposition as well as abetting electoral fraud. In 2003, the police were also an instrument used by the PDP to dislodge the AD in several states of the South-West.

The use of the police and other security agencies to intimidate the electorate in states not controlled by the PDP was evident in Ekiti State in June 2014 and in Osun State in August 2014. Both states were flooded with federal security agents ostensibly to maintain the peace. But the real motive was to suppress the vote of the APC whilst boosting that of the PDP. The experience of the Attorney-General and Commissioner of Justice of Osun State, Chief Wale Afolabi, was shocking and telling. Hooded security agents or fake agents of the Federal Government detained and arrested the Attorney-General and about two hundred APC members without any evidence of wrongdoing. As reported in *The Guardian* newspaper of September 9, 2014, neither the Attorney General nor the APC members arrested committed any crime. Because of the false arrest, the Commissioner and the others detained were not able to cast their ballots. Regrettably, these antics violated Nigerian laws and are a throwback to the events of 1962-1965. Use of security agencies to suppress the vote and commit electoral fraud makes a mockery of our democratic claim.

The first step in solving the myriad problems of Nigeria is to meet in a sovereign national conference elected by the people to agree to a new and truly federal structure. In such a federal state, each region will be able to develop at its own pace, curb crime in its region, entrench in its constitution peculiar cultural practices unique to its region. Of course, some may argue that a weak federal government will lead to the break-up of Nigeria. But let us reverse the argument. Has a strong and dominant central government, which was imposed by the military in January 1966, led to a safe, secure and united Nigeria? The answer is definitely **NO** as shown in the analysis above.

Switzerland is a confederation with a population of about seven and a half million people, yet it is thriving. Some European states which are known as united countries such as the United Kingdom of Great Britain and Northern Ireland, which constituent nations have been united for several centuries are rethinking the framework of their association.

For Nigeria to avoid such fate in the future, it has to adopt a genuine federal constitution that promotes regional autonomy and put in place and implement laws that will hold the leadership accountable. In addition, the regional and federal constitutions should create institutions that will promote good governance and state effectiveness. The attitude of Nigerians to non-performing governments must also change. Citizens should be prepared to defend their rights through a democratic process.

As I approach my ninetieth year, I pray that my descendants

will live to see a truly federal Nigeria that is able and is seen to be solving the several ills that plague the country. I pray for peace in all parts of Nigeria, for honest, transparent and accountable leadership and for institutions that will make all these possible. I pray for a Nigeria that is united because each of the many nations that constitute the country feels comfortable and confident to belong to Nigeria, not one where the rhetoric of unity crowds out the principle of justice and equality in a multinational federation. Amen.

A Short Introspection by Senator Ayo Fasanmi as he approached 91 years of age—(June 2016)

I thank God for giving me a long and healthy life. I also thank God for the children He gave me. Every day and especially today, I remember my late wife, Felicia Adejoke, who stood by me until her passing to the greater beyond. I thank God for giving me the strength to bear her loss. I acknowledge the help of my relations and the support of my political associates in the progressive movement.

Though trained as a pharmacist, most of my adult years have been devoted to politics. My interest and passion for politics began over 70 years ago. Since that beginning, I have been privileged to serve in the Federal Parliament as a member of the House of Representatives between 1964-1966, and a Senator from 1979-1983. In the Fourth Republic, I have been appointed as one of the elders of leading progressive parties such as the Alliance for Democracy which was succeeded by the Action

Congress of Nigeria. In old age, I am a strong supporter of the All Progressives Congress.

In all my years in politics, my goal, as well as those of many first-generation Nigerian politicians, was to serve, to improve the lives of our citizens, and in the motto of the Action Group to "make life more abundant".

The hope of my generation was that an independent Nigeria would achieve economic and social development rapidly given the attributes of our country, a large population, a variety of agricultural and mineral resources and hydrocarbons. Regrettably, that hope was dashed due to several factors: corruption, mismanagement, praetorian interventions in governance, and misplaced priorities.

Yet, we can lift ourselves up by becoming disciplined, eschewing corruption, fair play in political matters, and instituting appropriate policies. No state ever develops without discipline and elite restraint. Discipline starts with each of us. We have to imbibe and practice honesty, teach our children to be forthright and principled, avoid cheating either in school or employment place. The attributes of honesty, integrity should radiate to all sectors of our lives, be it in church, mosque, social groups and, of course, politics.

I mentioned earlier that corruption should be avoided. The consequences of corruption are apparent as it has stultified development of Nigeria and perverted its politics. There is no doubt that corruption and gross mismanagement are major factors in our underdevelopment. Indeed, were the funds siphoned off into private accounts available to the current administration,

Nigeria might have been able to cope with decline in our oil revenue.

Leadership at all levels must be transparent and accountable. Our leaders should be tolerant, avoid inflammatory statements that can lead to violence, and build bridges across ethnic groups, regions and religions. Further, our elected leaders should reduce their allowances in view of our economic situation, which regrettably is parlous. Above all, our political leaders should plan for the future and incorporate youths in all development plans. Youth unemployment which feeds crime and stunt hopes is worrisome. Consequently, the government and private sector should work together to address this and other gnawing problems.

I note and commend the President for his austere lifestyle. I also welcome the several programmes the federal government is unveiling to end the recession. We should all support the administration in the herculean task to strengthen the economy, curb corruption and impunity, and ensure security in all parts of Nigeria.

I thank you and pray for long life for all and pray for a stable democratic Federal Nigeria.

Senator Fasanmi Lauds Governors of South-West (January 2020)

The National leader of Yoruba sociocultural political organisation, Egbe Afenifere Ilosiwaju Yoruba, Senator Ayo Fasanmi has commended South-West Governors for their positive initiative to curb rampant insecurity in the region.

Senator Fasanmi, who was a lawmaker in the First and Second Republics, made the remarks in Osogbo through his Personal Assistant, Mr Temitope Adebayo. The Senator stressed that the good moves taken by the Governors of the South-West Region show that they are much concerned about the lives of the people they are governing.

Senator Fasanmi, the oldest, much revered, surviving Senator in the country, said that the regional security network, recently established in the South-West, is a good sign of collaboration on security which other regions in Nigeria should consider.

"Yorubas can speak with one voice when it comes to the development of the Region regardless of affiliations. That is laudable and heartening" he said.

Senator Ayo Fasanmi also pleaded with pertinent security agencies to work together in concretizing the creation of the OPERATION AMOTEKUN.

"This should become a salient reality in the Region." Senator Fasanmi said, "The Police, OPC, local hunters, and other security personnel who are attached to state governments should make sure that they do their jobs competently without compromise."

Senator Ayo Fasanmi further said that the opposition should not always sit on the fence and criticize the government but must learn to see the good side of the government. He exhorted: "It is time for Yorubas to come together and speak with one voice. If our Governors can do this, I believe all the other Yoruba leaders can do the same."

Senator Fasanmi went down memory lane to buttress his points. "When Papa Awolowo was alive, he used to tell us that it is not life that matters, but it is the courage every one of us brings to it that matters."

Senator Fasanmi reiterated that he is ready to contribute his own quota anytime his elderly advice is sought, adding that "I have been fighting for the unity of this Nation from an early age in life. I fervently wish the Governors under the leadership of His Excellency, Rotimi Akeredolu, a successful deliberation with positive light at the end of the tunnel."

Senator Fasanmi's New Year Message to Afenifere Leaders (January 2020)

The National Leader of Yoruba Socio-cultural Group, Egbe Afenifere, Senator Ayo Fasanmi has urged all Yorubas irrespective of affiliations and beliefs to join hands together to fight injustice across the region.

In a statement released to the press in Osogbo by his Personal Assistant, Mr. Temitope Adebayo, the Senator said that the forthcoming meeting of Afenifere on the 21st of January is a crucial one which should be attended by every leader who holds dear the ideals of Afenifere.

The Senator stressed that "When it comes to the development of the region, we must unite and speak with one voice. With this in mind, I have personally conducted a series of consultations with a lot of Yoruba leaders who are not only stakeholders, but are also visionaries."

Pertaining to security in the South-West, Senator Fasanmi said, "I am particularly pleased with the steps our Governors are taking in this regard. Our Governors are not acting against the law, rather, they are acting in the interest of their people. They are, indeed, "Chief Security Officers" and "Gatekeepers" of their states.

Egbe Afenifere Ilosiwaju Yoruba (January, 2020)

I seize this opportunity to welcome every one of you to the first meeting in the year 2020. I am also wishing everybody a prosperous and meritorious new year.

Before I present my address, it would constitute an ungrateful attitude if I fail to show my appreciation for the epochal 94th birthday which you organised for me on September 26, 2019. It was an event which I can never forget in the journey of my political life. I thank you and I wish everyone of you a long life, I pray that all of you shall be celebrated at your old age in Jesus' name.

If not because of my old age and health challenges, I would have loved to pay a series of courtesy visits to individuals.

All our leaders from each state are wonderful. However, because of time constraints, I shall not be able to recognize you one by one but I seek your permission to recognize some of our respected leaders: Senator Biyi Durojaiye, Prince Tajudeen Olusi, Elder Yemi Alade, Chief S.M. Akindele, Excellency Sooko Adeleke Adewoyin, all the representatives of several state governments present, our National Secretary and all the dedicated members of Egbe Afenifere Ilosiwaju Yoruba.

Afenifere is a living vision of our great leader, Obafemi Awolowo. It is a socio-cultural political organisation. It serves as an arm of our progressive party and people who have passion for progressive ideals. Some people have dropped progressive vision due to self-interest.

Let me end my short statement by quoting Chief Awolowo, who admonished us to always remain firm like an anvil being stricken. He said further that "it is not life that matters but the courage which every one of us brings to it that matters".

Young Ayo Fasanmi (standing second left) with other members of the Government College Ibadan Football Team in 1944

Senator Fasanmi's family picture was taken on his 25th wedding anniversary in 1978 in Iye-Ekiti. From left to right: Late Ayorinde Jnr, Folake, Olufunmilayo, Senator Fasanmi, Chief (Mrs) Felicia Adejoke Fasanmi, Afolabi, Olufunke and Obafemi.

Ayo Fasanmi speaking at a political rally in 1964

Fasanmi (sitting 5th from right) with other members of the Action Group Youth Association in 1965

Nigeria-Soviet Friendship Society represented by Ayo Fasanmi (2nd left) along with Mr. Nathaniel Anah and Mr. Anthony Iheagwam on a visit to the Soviet Union in 1965.

Chief Ayo Fasanmi (2nd right) with Chief Obafemi Awolowo speaking at an event after the latter's release from prison in 1966

Chief Obafemi Awolowo (left) at the 25th wedding anniversary of Chief & Chief (Mrs.) Ayo Fasanmi in 1978.

Chief Fasanmi (right) as President of Pharmaceutical Society of Nigeria at the National Conference of the Society in 1977.

Chief Fasanmi welcoming the then Military Governor of Oyo State, Brigadier David A. Jemibewon to the National Conference of Pharmaceutical Society of Nigeria in 1977.

Senator Fasanmi with Senator Abraham Adesanya (middle) at the 1977 Constituent Assembly.

Senator Fasanmi with Dr. Tunji Otegebeye (first left) and Chief Richard Akinjide (middle) at the Constituent Assembly in 1977.

Senator Fasanmi with other Alliance for Democracy (AD) party members at its National Convention in Abuja in 2000

Senator Ayo Fasanmi with Professor Bayonile Ademodi (first left) at an Alliance for Democracy event.

Senator Fasanmi addressing participants at the Yoruba Youth Leadership Summit held in Lagos in honour of his 90th birthday in September 2015.

Senator Fasanmi, with President Muhammad Buhari (second left), Vice-President Yemi Osinbajo (first right) and Governor Fayemi (first left) during a 2019 APC Presidential campaign stop at Ado-Ekiti.

Senator Fasanmi (standing next to President Muhammadu Buhari) led a delegation of Yoruba leaders to Abuja to protest the killings of Yorubas at the hands of Fulani herdsmen in August 2019.

Senator Fasanmi with Governor of Ekiti State, Dr. Kayode Fayemi (in the middle) and Professor Banji Akintoye, at a political event in January 2020.

Senator Fasanmi with Governor of Osun State, Gov Adegboyega Oyetola at a reception held in honour of eminent Osun State personalities in January 2020.

Senator Fasanmi with members of Osun State Chapter of Pharmaceutical Society who paid him a courtesy visit at his Osogbo residence in March 2020.

The Ayo Fasanmi Model College Ilokun, Ado-Ekiti named in his honour by Governor Kayode Fayemi and commissioned in October 2020.

Senator Fasanmi's son Obafemi Fasanmi (standing next to the Senator) was sworn in as a High Court Judge in Ekiti State on January 8, 2020. The Senator said witnessing his son being sworn in as a Judge was the happiest day in his life.

CHAPTER FOUR

TRIBUTES

This chapter is a compilation of selected tributes to Senator Ayo Fasanmi on his passing on July 29, 2020. The tributes were extracted from his funeral programme, newspapers and social media.

Tributes started pouring in as soon as the news of the passing of Senator Ayo Fasanmi broke on July 29, 2020, three months shy of his 95th birthday, after a very brief illness. The news was broadcast over radio and television stations as well as social media websites. Most of the tributes recorded in this chapter were from his political allies and some from political opponents. These tributes would make a book on their own if they were all published, but for brevity, we decided to select a few in their verbatim form while making do with just extracts from others.

The tributes reflect the reach of his engagement and

willingness to collaborate with political opponents to achieve political goals he deemed would promote a progressive agenda; an agenda that he pursued consistently through his lifetime.

Until his passing, Chief Fasanmi, despite advanced age, participated in and attended many political and social events, the most important of which was the swearing-in of his son, Obafemi Fasanmi, as a Judge in Ekiti State on January 8, 2020. He described the day as the happiest in his life.

Other activities in January 2020, included attendance at a dinner party organised by APC to celebrate the Supreme Court judgement which upheld the election of Governor Adegboyega Oyetola as Osun State Governor. The Senator hosted the Afenifere Renewal Group at his residence in Osogbo in late January.

In February, he travelled to Ado-Ekiti to congratulate Governor Fayemi on the occasion of his 55th birthday. In the same month, he led the delegation of Osun State Chapter of Afenifere to the Osun State Governor.

In March, he hosted the Osun State Chapter of the Pharmaceutical Society of Nigeria (PSN) in his Osogbo residence. On that occasion, the Osun State Chapter of the PSN presented him an award in recognition of his commitment to the Society. Later in March, the newly installed Oba, Oore of Otun Ekiti, came to visit and to express his appreciation for the role the late Senator played in his installation.

Now follow the tributes, the first one in the compilation being from the nation's President:

Muhammadu Buhari, President of the Federal Republic of Nigeria

The following statement was issued by Femi Adesina, Special Adviser on Media and Publicity to The President of the Federal Republic of Nigeria.

President Muhammadu Buhari joins Yoruba sociocultural and political organisation, Afenifere, in mourning the passing of Pa Ayorinde Fasanmi, describing his death "as a big loss to the nation"

The President condoles with people and government of Osun and Ekiti States, family members, friends and associates of the elder statesman, who served as a legislator in both Houses of Representatives and Senate and distinguished himself politically by always standing for the truth, especially on issues related to the uplifting of the downtrodden.

President Buhari affirms that Chief Fasanmi's wise counsels borne out of humility, deep reflection, diligent studies and experience will be sorely missed by governments at different levels, as he regularly listened to leaders, and always had good advice on going forward.

As an ardent follower of the late sage, Chief Obafemi Awolowo, the President believes the fearless and consistent leader of the sociocultural and political organisation lived to serve his people and the nation, and the progressive ideals that he projected impacted greatly and provided a road map on development at state and federal levels.

President Buhari notes, with commendation, that the efforts of Chief Fasanmi in the founding and sustenance of Nigeria's democracy will be remembered, and posterity will be glad for his great sacrifices.

The President prays that the Almighty God will receive the soul of the departed leader, and comfort his family.

Goodluck Jonathan, former President of Nigeria

Former President Goodluck Jonathan has commiserated with the government and people of Osun State as well as the family of the late leader of the Yoruba sociocultural organisation, Afenifere, Pa Ayorinde Fasanmi, describing his death as a great loss to the nation. The statement was issued by Ikechukwu Eze, the former President's Media Adviser.

The former President's statement noted further that Fasanmi was an exemplary patriot and nationalist who fought for Nigeria's independence, adding that he continued to fight for the welfare of Nigerians until the last days of his life.

Jonathan also commended the late Fasanmi's loyalty to the Nigerian cause, stressing that he was a national hero whose love for his people and country knew no bounds.

"Pa Fasanmi's spirited crusade for freedom, equity and justice spanned generations. As a young man he joined forces with his mentor, the late Chief Obafemi Awolowo, and other formidable nationalists to fight for our nation's independence and remained a force for fairness, unity, democracy, and good governance until his death.

He will be remembered for his exceptional democratic credentials, inimitable candour and selflessness."

Yemi Osinbajo, Vice-President of the Federal Republic of Nigeria

We received the news of the passing of Papa, Senator Ayo Fasanmi, with deep sadness and grief.

Pa Fasanmi belonged to that breed of Nigerian leaders who were irrevocably committed to the upliftment and welfare of the Nigerian people. He took the opportunity of leadership and political office as truly a call to serve.

Recently, while reflecting on his participation in public life he said "we were out to fight against diseases and poverty, as well as to ensure that the common man did not become the wretched of the earth."

A founding leader of Afenifere, a true patriot, a forthright servant, an interlocutor for the common man has passed on.

A man of deep conviction who remained loyal to the end to compatriots and colleagues in the progressive tendency from the Action Group (AG) to the All Progressives Congress (APC), now enters into eternity.

We thank God for giving him to us for 94 years. His legacy of consistency in egalitarian beliefs, social justice, and action lives on.

We extend our heartfelt condolences to all members of the

family and Papa's associates.

We also commiserate with the governments and people of Ekiti State, his home State, and Osun State where he lived for most of his adult life until his death.

May the Lord comfort us all and bless his memory always.

Atiku Abubakar, former Vice-President of Nigeria

A one-time Vice President of Nigeria, Atiku Abubakar took to his official Twitter account to pay homage to Chief Fasanmi whom he described as a selfless man who had the restoration of democracy in the country at heart.

His tweet reads:

"Chief Ayo Fasanmi belonged in the elite club of the founding fathers of our country. He was also actively involved in the push for the restoration of democracy. He will be sorely missed. My thoughts and prayers are with his family. May God Almighty grant his soul eternal rest.—AA"

Bola Tinubu, National APC Leader

Papa Fasanmi Devoted Himself Toward Progressive Development & Democratic Advancement

Papa Ayo Fasanmi's long sojourn on earth was for the good of all. He walked at the vanguard of all democrats, freedom fighters, and believers in true federalism. To have lived to the age of 94 was God's gift not only to him, but to this nation he loved so deeply. Senator Fasanmi was an eminent politician, elder statesman and the beloved leader of Afenifere.

A colourful personality, Papa was principled, courageous and honest. He was a loyal and dependable ally of the indomitable Chief Obafemi Awolowo. For all his life, Pa Fasanmi practised and advanced the virtues he learned at the feet of his leader. He never betrayed those values.

Like the American civil rights leader and Congressman John Lewis, who was recently buried, Papa Fasanmi remained faithful to the truth for which he suffered greatly. Yet, no matter the cost, he never strayed from his principles. A brave man, he never flinched at the prospect of speaking truth to power.

I had a close relationship with Papa Fasanmi, dating back many years. He was a mentor and role model to me, and many others who believe in progressive politics as a means to uplift our society and its people. When Papa was recently admitted to hospital for age-related sickness, I spoke to him and followed up with his close aide to monitor his situation.

As Afenifere leader, he was a true believer in the importance of fiscal federalism as essential for the growth of Nigeria. His vision for our nation was a coherent and correct one.

I commiserate with the family, associates and progressives throughout our country, the South-West and Ekiti State. With Papa's passing, we have lost someone special and excellent in every way.

I also share in the grief of this moment with his political soulmates, Pa Fasoranti, Chief Bisi Akande, and others. I commiserate with Ekiti State Governor Kayode Fayemi and Governor Adegboyega Oyetola of Osun State who was in regular contact with Papa, for the late Senator resided in Osogbo where he spent 70 years of his life, and maintained a Chemist Store named Bamidupe Chemist.

Papa Fasanmi devoted himself toward progressive development and democratic advancement. This fine job has not been completed. The Nigeria of our dreams is still a work in progress. Papa struggled for that dream and supported those patriots, like President Muhammad Buhari, who also toiled for the same goal. Let us all learn from Papa Fasanmi's example and join hands to move Nigeria towards the safe harbour of peace and prosperity.

As Papa's remains are being buried today, we pray that Almighty God grant his soul eternal rest. May God also guide and comfort his family that they may have the strength and perseverance to continue after him through living his example. God bless Nigeria.

Ahmad Lawan, The Senate President

Senate President, Ahmad Lawan, has commiserated with the family, friends and political associates of Pa Ayorinde Fasanmi, the leader of Yoruba sociocultural and political association who died on Wednesday at the age of 94 years.

Lawan also commiserated with the government and people of Ekiti state and the Yoruba people in general over the demise of a leader, who throughout his life, was committed to the cause of his people and Nigeria.

The Senate President said the late elder statesman "made

immense contributions to nation-building as a two-time parliamentarian, public office holder and political party leader." Lawan said "Nigerians will miss Pa Fasanmi's forthrightness, consistency, wise counsel and wealth of experience.

He prayed to God to grant the soul of the deceased perfect peace and grant those that he left behind the fortitude to bear his loss.

Femi Gbajabiamila, Speaker of the House of Representatives, Federal Republic of Nigeria

In a statement by his Special Adviser on Media and Publicity, Lanre Lasisi, the Speaker said though the demise of the late patriot would be felt by the nation, the progressives, and his family, solace would, however, be taken in the fact that his footprints have been firmly entrenched in the sands of time.

The Speaker also noted that Pa Fasanmi's passionate quest for democracy and good governance saw him leave pharmacy to join politics and later became the leader of the Yoruba sociocultural group, Afenifere.

As a Federal lawmaker at the national level, first as a member of the House of Representatives and later a Senator, Pa Fasanmi came across as a symbol of humility, selflessness and integrity, which have continued to inspire lawmakers across the country.

Kayode Fayemi, Governor of Ekiti State

The death of Chief Ayorinde Fasanmi, on July 29, 2020 has reinforced the saying that no matter how long we live, our time here remains transient. Even though Baba Ayo Fasanmi died at an advanced age of 94 years, his death is a monumental and personal loss to me. As the African adage says, "the death of an elder in Africa is like a library set on fire." This aphorism is much truer with the fallen socialist ideologue and Ekiti Elder. Even in his advanced age, Chief Ayo Fasanmi had a mind as sharp as the razor and photographic memory of past events with undiluted clarity. He was a living library in Nigeria's political history, wisdom, knowledge, and native intelligence.

His death has, therefore, robbed me of a godfather, counsellor, and advocate and a father. A good man has left us. We will sorely miss him, but we are consoled that Baba's entire adult life was dedicated to selfless service. He lived his life in the fear of God and for the advancement of humanity. He joins two other prominent Ekiti icons who recently went the way of the ancestors: Evangelist Bamidele Isola Olumilua, Pa S. K. Babalola and Sir Oluremi Omotoso. In the space of three months, Ekiti has lost some of our most invaluable elders and statesmen.

Born in Lagos in 1925, to a struggling family of an Iye-Ekiti father and an Ijero-Ekiti mother, Chief Ayo Fasanmi's early life was wrought in the furnace of struggles. He had an almost blighted beginning that blurred a possibility of a great future before him. Although he enrolled in the primary school at St Paul, Ebute-Meta in 1935, he had to abandon his education only to return to it in 1937 at St. Marks, Offa, Kwara State, through the long arm of providence. By the time he finished his primary education in 1941, he was the only candidate who passed his common entrance, a feat which earned him a scholarship to study in Government College, Ibadan. He passed out in 1947 and got admitted to the School of Pharmacy, Yaba later in 1947, he finished his training in Pharmacy in 1950 and was posted to Osogbo and he had since then made the town his home. It was in Osogbo that his path crossed with my Dad's who was a civil servant—a Public Enlightenment Officer—a relationship that endured till my Dad's demise in 2009.

Since my coming to politics, Baba has been a tremendous pillar of support. He was a dependable, reliable, unwavering, and consistent mentor, leader and ally. Hardly a week passed by in my last fifteen years in partisan politics without an exchange between us. He was a fearless man who courageously expressed himself without minding whose ox was gored. He would give without asking. He was a stabiliser and one to run to in the moment of crisis.

One legacy for which Baba would be fondly remembered was his credential of incorruptibility. He was a man of tall integrity and honesty. It would be recalled that he was the first to start the Anti-Bribery and Anti-Corruption Committee in 1972 under Colonel Oluwole Rotimi of the Western Region. He would go round roads and highways to arrest police and other enforcement agents who were collecting bribes on the roads, in his determined commitment to stamp out corruption in Nigeria.

One event that further bore eloquent testimony to his high integrity quotient was the 1994 Constitutional Conference debacle, when the Yoruba nation spoke with one voice that all Yoruba delegates serving in the Constitutional Conference of

General Abacha, should return home, Chief Ayo Fasanmi, was one of the reliable compatriots who heeded the call and joined hands with his brothers to form NADECO to push for the end to military rule. He is one of the unsung heroes of our democratic struggle and one that we should never forget his immense sacrifices to national development. He always held fervently that the things he would want to be remembered for were to be seen as a committed Awoist, a man of integrity and a man who fought for the cause of the downtrodden. He never failed in them. He remained a committed Awoist till death and defended the good name of the sage at every opportunity.

I deeply appreciate the invaluable support and unconditional love that Baba showed me. He must have visited me more than three times this year alone. He ceaselessly called to offer advice and provided leadership whenever occasions demanded.

As a token of appreciation to his contribution to the development of Ekiti, Nigeria and humanity, and particularly for being an embodiment of the finest Ekiti values, my government named one of the newly created secondary schools after him. I am glad we did this during his lifetime. My only regret was that he has now left us before the school will be officially inaugurated for academic activities when schools finally reopen.

Chief Ayo Fasanmi has come, has seen, and has conquered. He conquered human cravings, vanity of power, ostentation, greed, and malice. He was a man of simple taste, amiable, peaceable, and selfless. He jealously guarded his reputation and lived within his means. He was a man of peace and a balanced arbiter who enjoyed the confidence of everyone around him.

As one of the first generation of trained pharmacists, Chief

Ayo Fasanmi personified pharmacy practice. It was a profession he practised all his life and to which he was totally committed. He was a former Chairman of Pharmaceutical Society of Nigeria, Oyo State, for many years before he became the President of the Society in 1977-1979. He became a Fellow of the Society in 1984 and remained a major figure within the Society.

He was a devout Christian whose Christianity manifested in the judicious manner he related with everyone he encountered. Until his death, he was the Baba Ijo of St. John Anglican Church, Iye-Ekiti and one of the patrons of All Souls Cathedral Osogbo where he worshipped for most of his life.

He was a proud Ekiti man, a faithful husband to his late wife, Late Madam Adejoke Fasanmi to whom he had married since 1953, until she passed away in 2014. Baba had determined that both of them would be buried in the same grave, to sleep on each other till eternity. Even in death, he remained committed to the love of his life!

Adieu, Baba Ayorinde Fasanmi, a quintessential Ekiti elder, a distinguished pharmacist and a dogged fighter, an astute politician, a devout Christian, and a loving family man.

We will continue to raise the banner of service in the progressive tradition that you and your peers have bequeathed us.

He will be fondly remembered for his integrity to the progressive politics.

On behalf of my wife, government, and good people of Ekiti State, I hereby express my sincere condolences to his family and the entire people of Iye-Ekiti. May his gentle soul rest in peace.

"O di gboose Baba, o da'rinako, o do'ju ala, o tun do'ju orun k'ato ri ra wa".

Adegboyega Oyetola, Governor of Osun State

Pa Ayo Fasanmi: An undiluted progressive (1925-2020)

As Mother Earth receives one of its best donations to humanity today, I pay tribute to a dyed-in-the wool progressive who lived his life for the betterment of humanity. Service is second nature to the late Pa Fasanmi. His training as a pharmacist prepared him for selfless service to humanity and he wasted no time in faithfully transferring it to the larger business of politics.

Pa Ayo Fasanmi conscientiously promoted, projected and lived for the principles and legacies of the late Chief Obafemi Awolowo till he breathed his last.

In his 94 years on earth, Pa Fasanmi proved that loving and serving Nigeria passionately and without personal benefits is doable. He was one of few patriarchs who stood to be counted in a nation in search of politics of ideology and principle. Throughout his foray into politics, he was consistent as a progressive.

Despite losing to a colleague, Pa Adekunle Ajasin, in the Unity Party of Nigeria's gubernatorial primary election in 1978, he remained a committed party man and worked for the success of the party's candidate.

Pa Fasanmi was a distinguished son of Ekiti who found a home in the State of Osun and worked tirelessly for the progress of the Yoruba race as an Afenifere leader. Every 30 minutes at Pa Fasanmi's feet was more than reading scores of books on politics.

Pa Fasanmi was a passionate believer in a better Nigeria. He was ever seeking to enrich and expand the frontiers of sociopolitical knowledge, encourage mass political participation, and offer selfless service to build a successor generation.

Pa Fasanmi's life, times and legacy typify the Omoluabi ethos that the State of Osun holds dear. Despite his advanced age, he was a regular face at all Osun programmes and would offer sincere counsel for the growth of the State.

Pa Fasanmi was a beacon of hope for a new Nigeria and an encouragement to the younger generation of politicians and public administrators.

It is unfortunate that he died at a time we were all looking forward to celebrating his 95th birthday and tapping more from his fountain of knowledge and experience. No doubt, his death is a colossal loss not only to Osun where he lived until his death, or Ekiti where he hailed from, but also to the entire country and the black race. He will be greatly missed.

The Government and People of Osun celebrate a father and a leader of monumental significance and pray to God to keep and strengthen the family he left behind.

Rest in peace, Pa Fasanmi.

Babajide Sanwo-Olu, Governor of Lagos State

It is with immense sadness that I learnt about the demise of Senator Ayo Fasanmi, who passed away on July 29, 2020 at the age of 94 years.

Senator Fasanmi was undoubtedly a great nationalist, passionate leader and champion of a true Nigeria that would work for every citizen. Pa Fasanmi was a complete gentleman, selfless and exemplary leader who spent the greater part of his life in the service of humanity, particularly the emancipation of the Yoruba people, the development of the region in particular and the nation in general.

Pa Fasanmi stood firmly behind the practice of constitutional democracy, fiscal federalism as a basis for sustainable development and lifting of the masses out of poverty. He was indeed an icon that will never be forgotten in the history of Nigeria and the Yoruba race in particular. He will be sorely missed.

On a personal note, I recall with admiration and affection how I closely followed and admired the late Pa Fasanmi. His words of wisdom, his principled position as leader of Afenifere and his capacity to speak truth to power will remain indelible in the annals of political history in Nigeria.

On behalf of my family and the good people of Lagos State, I want to express sincere and heartfelt condolences to late Pa Fasanmi's family, friends and associates. May God grant the departed soul eternal rest and the family the fortitude to bear the irreparable loss.

Adieu Papa!

Dapo Abiodun, Governor of Ogun State

Passage of Senator Ayo Fasanmi: Loss of a consummate nationalist

I received the sad news of the passage of Senator Ayo Fasanmi on Wednesday 29 July, 2020 with deep pain and grief. On behalf of my family, the Government and the good people of Ogun State, I convey our deepest condolences.

His demise not only denies you the companionship of

a loving and affectionate father, but further diminishes the rank of elder statesmen and progressives, whose wisdom and guidance are needed as a compass to navigate our ways out of various national challenges. Pa Fasanmi was both a political and professional phenomenon. He was a symbol of fidelity to social welfarist ideology and a pharmacist of great standing that attained the peak of his career as the National President of the Pharmaceutical Society of Nigeria in 1977.

His contributions to national development threw him up as not only a leader of Afenifere, the pan-Yoruba sociocultural organisation, but as a national hero, Papa served in both Houses of the National Assembly—the House of Representatives and later in the Senate—and also served as a member of National Constitutional Conference Commission in 1994. This is unprecedented. His death is a very sad loss, indeed. But we cannot question God for calling him at this time. He will be sorely missed.

Our solace lies in the fact that Papa Fasanmi lived a fulfilled life of honesty, integrity, courage and commitment to the development of our common patrimony that should be emulated by the oncoming generation. He will always be adored by most of us.

Certainly, posterity will accord him his due recognition for his legacies of service and forthrightness.

While appreciating the life and times of this great consensus builder and stabilising factor in our political firmament, I pray that the Almighty repose his soul and grant the family, friends and associates the fortitude to bear this painful loss.

Once again, please accept our heartfelt condolences and the

assurance of my warmest regards, as always.

Oluwarotimi Akeredolu, Governor of Ondo State

Tribute to our departed icon: Senator Ayo Fasanmi

It is with mixed feelings that we celebrate the exit of one of the few remaining old, tested and committed leaders of Yorubaland. Pa Fasanmi devoted his youthful existence to the service of his fatherland. He remained truthful till the end. Posterity already reserves an enviable space for him in the pantheon of our ancestors.

Papa saw it all. Starting from political pupilage under the late sage, Awo, in the pre-independence era, our departed nationalist represented the people of Ekiti of the former Western Region in the House of Representatives during the First Republic. Thereafter, he returned to his profession, Pharmacy, during the interregnum until the return to civil rule in 1979. Great and unshaken was the trust in Papa Fasanmi that he was also voted to represent the same people in the Senate between 1979 and 1983.

He remained one of the very dedicated apostles of the late sage in words and deeds. He joined others to resist prolonged military rule. He followed the progressive principles upon which the foundation of politics was laid in the South-West. He decided to take the back seat after the return to civil rule in 1999, though he was not tired still. He continued to make meaningful contributions at crucial moments in the polity.

We must not shy away from mentioning the fact of his quiet, impactful and significant interventions in our recent sociopolitical experiences. He was not afraid to speak truth to power; but he appreciated the volatility of the issues of the moment and, like a good elder, whose presence in the public space compels rectitude, he chose the most appropriate and effective medium to speak on behalf of his people. He never failed to pitch his tent with his people, even when it was most inexpedient.

He was not a partisan of injustice and not a parochial political practitioner for self aggrandisement. He was not scared of standing alone or of pernicious labelling. Once convinced of the justness of the cause, Pa Fasanmi was the man who would take the plunge without looking back. It is, therefore, not surprising that he was very active until he breathed his last, when those who were far younger would employ the instrumentality of age to promote cowardice, perfidy and avarice.

He was a man who believed in peace. He was, however, not scared of conflict in the defense of justice. He did not allow age to mellow his activities even when this could be used as a weapon for inaction and sabotage. He was bold and decent. He liked to remember the past and drew useful lessons therefrom. He was a true leader in whom there was no guile. He was indeed a man of honour.

We have lost a true patriot: a father to the Yoruba nation who gave his best in the service of all of us. The implication of his death to the Yoruba nation is deep and far reaching: we have lost one of our respectable voices.

Adieu to the great Awoist.

Bisi Akande, Former Governor of Osun State

"Tribute to my political godfather Pa Ayo Fasanmi"

I'm suddenly made a political orphan by the passing of Papa Ayo Fasanmi at this point. It is shocking and very painful to me personally because he was my political godfather since he introduced me to Chief Obafemi Awolowo in 1977.

I am sure his passing is a great loss to the Yoruba nation and to Nigeria as a whole.

Papa Fasanmi, along with his leader Chief Obafemi Awolowo, was in the Regional House of Assembly and National House of Representatives during the Parliamentary system of Government in the Nigerian First Republic and he became a Senator of the Federal Republic of Nigeria in the Presidential system of Government in the Second Republic. We were together in the National Constituent Assembly that wrote the 1979 Constitution for Nigeria. His wealth of experience as a progressive politician is mostly needed now that Nigeria is gradually taking steps towards consolidating democratic norms, hence a big vacuum has been created by his exit.

Those Nigerians that were not born before 1966 would only have the military sense of democracy and may never know good governance unless they were fortunate to have learnt under the tutelage of people of Papa Fasanmi's political generation. It is significant, therefore, that the knowledge of the contributions of Fasanmi's generation to the development of Nigeria become useful for thinking right on how to reposition the problems of Nigeria.

He had consistently been a champion of democracy and good

governance which he pursued till he breathed his last. His role in ensuring Yoruba has a place of its own in the politics of Nigeria will remain indelible while his contributions to the formation and sustenance of Afenifere, the pan-Yoruba sociopolitical organisation, cannot be ignored.

Papa Fasanmi will be sorely missed by us, his political associates and by the entire nation.

May God grant him eternal rest as we pray to God to give us, family, friends, political associates fortitude to bear the irreparable loss.

Rauf Aregbesola, Hon. Minister of Interior and former Governor of Osun State

Fasanmi: A Titan Gone

I received with shock, but submission to the will of God, the news of the passage of Senator Ayorinde Fasanmi, which occurred on Wednesday July 29, 2020. He was 94 years old. The titan is gone!

Pa Fasanmi was the ideal Nigerian and quintessential Yoruba Omoluabi. He trained and practised as a pharmacist and rose to the pinnacle of the profession when he was elected the National President of Pharmaceutical Society of Nigeria in 1977. But he emerged from the cocoon of the pharmaceutical industry into national limelight in 1979 when he was elected into the Nigerian Senate of the short-lived Second Republic. Before then, he had been in the House of Representatives in the First Republic. He was also a delegate to the Constitutional Conference of 1994.

Though a native of Iye-Ekiti in Ekiti State, he lived his

adult life in Osogbo, where he took permanent residence and was well regarded as a leader. He would be counted among those instrumental for the creation of the State of Osun in 1991 and never ceased from working for its development till he died.

Pa Fasanmi was a progressive to the core and never deviated from the mission to enthrone a democratic, egalitarian, just, fair and prosperous order in our society. He was a close associate and disciple of Chief Obafemi Awolowo. He drank from his fountain of knowledge, wisdom and conception of political power as an instrument of service to the public. He lived and breathed this credo all his life.

As a leader of Afenifere, he fought for the restoration of the June 12, 1993 Presidential Electoral Mandate of Chief Moshood Abiola and was visited with much retribution by the regimes of General Ibrahim Babangida and Sani Abacha on account of this. He bore it with stoicism and equanimity. His core was made of alloy, so to speak, making him unbending to the carrot or stick of dictators.

His integrity was transparent and infectious. He had the uncommon grace to have witnessed first-hand Nigeria's political development—from the anti-colonial struggles, the First Republic, the first military interregnum and the civil war, the short-lived Second Republic, the second military era, the stillborn Third Republic, the third military rule and the break of the Fourth Republic in 1999 till date.

He was a living encyclopaedia of Nigeria government and politics and repository of events lasting nearly a century of his sojourn on the face of the earth. We have irretrievably lost a national asset. His death is very devastating and a personal loss to me. He was one of the Yoruba elders and leaders of our party I consulted and who encouraged me to contest the 2007 governorship election.

He was of great assistance to me in winning the election and stood by me through the nearly four years it took to retrieve my mandate and was a strong pillar of our eight-year administration in Osun. His wise counsel, admonition, guidance and rebuke (when necessary), I found to be invaluable. My last physical encounter with him was in September last year when the State Government hosted me to a warm reception, following my appointment as minister.

He came to honour me with his presence and spoke well about me and his pleasure in my appointment and opportunity to serve at the national level. He lived a life of unalloyed service to humanity, Nigeria and the Yoruba race. He has left a gaping void difficult to fill. We will sorely miss him.

On behalf of my wife and our other associates, I offer the deepest condolences to his family, the governments and people of Osun and Ekiti States, his friends and associates.

May the Almighty God repose his soul and give him comfort in his next station.

Amen.

Niyi Adebayo, former Governor of Ekiti State and Hon Minister of Industry and Trade

I received with a mixture of sadness and joy the news of the passing on to glory of our dear Papa, Senator Ayo Fasanmi. Sadness because of the loss of a beloved father and political leader, but also of gratitude because he lived a fulfilled and fruitful life.

I eulogise the life and leadership virtues of our political leader, the late Senator Ayo Fasanmi. Papa will be greatly missed for his words of wisdom, leadership by example, a good life full of enviable legacies and his meritorious service to Yorubaland and Nigeria at large.

I fondly recall how Papa joined other patriots to stand on the side of ordinary Nigerians during the era of military junta and how he later contributed meaningfully to the enthronement of the Fourth Republic. This is the time that we would truly have benefitted from his wealth of experience to steer the affairs of our great nation to greater heights.

I also fondly recall how supportive Papa was to my election as Governor of Ekiti State in 1999, and throughout my tenure of office. He was also there for me politically afterwards. A very close friend of my late father, he remained true till the end and never stayed away from the Adebayo family after his friend's demise.

No doubt, we his political students will miss him, and I use this sober moment to urge the current crop of leaders in the country to emulate the political maturity, selflessness and dedication to national goals that our Afenifere leader represented and stood for during his lifetime.

For me, it is a celebration of life beautified with many landmark political achievements.

It is my fervent prayer that God will repose his soul, bless and protect both the immediate and political family he has left behind.

Segun Oni, former Governor of Ekiti State

Pa Ayo Fasanmi's incorruptible lifestyle worthy of emulation
The statement reads: "A luminous epoch in sociopolitical crusading has come to a dignifying end with the passing of elder statesman, Senator Ayo Fasanmi. But we take solace in the comforting truth that our highly revered father played his enviable part in the sociocultural and political development of Yorubaland before his transition to eternal rest in the bosom of our Lord and Saviour, Jesus Christ.

Senator Ayo Fasanmi was a lawmaker par excellence who served our country meritoriously; a foremost nationalist who lived an incorruptible lifestyle worthy of emulation; a courageous leader whose role was invaluable to the NADECO struggle; and a political activist who was one of the last set of survivors of the first order in the post-independence era.

My family and I offer our deepest condolences to the immediate family of Pa Fasanmi, even though his passing was a glorious exit that must be celebrated by all and sundry.

I take consolation in a life well-lived, and in also knowing that in his departure, we can all aspire to live by his ideals of selfless service, patriotism, and celebrate the end of a very eventful, dedicated, illustrious and industrious life," the statement added.

Gbenga Daniel, former Governor of Ogun State

A legacy of sincerity and forthrightness
The exit of Pa Ayo Fasanmi no doubt will leave a

conspicuous gap in the struggle for the identity of the Yoruba nation; his contribution to the emergence of the South-West region's political brand will be sorely missed.

Pa Fasanmi distinguished himself as a pharmacist of note and took his legacy of sincerity and forthrightness into the politics of the nation where he represented the people of Ondo North as an elected Senator in the Second Republic, and later in the Fourth Republic serving as the National Vice-Chairman Alliance for Democracy, South-West Zone.

In his 94 years, he joined others to provide leadership for the Yoruba nation, offering productive advice and valuable mentorship to many of the younger generation.

I am proud to be associated with him politically. His death is a personal loss to me because with him I share a common bond in the struggle for the cultural renaissance of the Yorubas in an emerging nation like Nigeria.

His exit is a great loss as we would have chosen to still have him around at this most auspicious time when Nigeria is in search of an identity and the Yoruba nation is expected to play a decisive role.

My heart goes out to his entire family, the Yoruba nation, Governors of the states of the South-West, leaders and members of Afenifere, for the sad loss of another icon of the Yoruba race.

Peter Obi, former Governor of Anambra State

A former governor of Anambra State, Mr. Peter Obi, has expressed sadness over the death of a leader of Yoruba sociopolitical group, Afenifere, Ayo Fasanmi who reportedly died on July 29.

Condoling with the Fasanmi Family, the government and people of Osun State, and the entire Afenifere group, Obi described Pa Fasanmi as a national leader and respected politician, who made landmark achievements in different levels of government.

The Northern Governors' Forum

In another development, the Northern Governors' Forum has mourned the death of elder statesman and leader of the Yoruba sociocultural group, Afenifere, Pa Ayorinde Fasanmi.

Governor Lalong, in a condolence message, on behalf of the Forum described the death of the elder statesman as a great loss to the Yoruba nation and Nigeria as a whole, given his enormous contributions to the political development of Nigeria.

Lalong said Pa Fasanmi played an active role in the enthronement of democracy and its sustenance through his roles as a legislator in the first and second Republics where he advocated for good governance, justice and equity.

While praying to God to grant his soul eternal rest, he condoled with his family, friends, political associates and followers.

The Middle Belt Forum

The Middle Belt Forum (MBF) has expressed shock at the death of Pa Ayo Fasanmi, who the Forum described as a true nationalist of repute.

The Forum noted that the death of Pa Ayo Fasanmi, a reputable champion of justice and progress for Nigerians, has robbed Nigeria's ethnic nationalities in the demand for restructuring for a better country founded on true federalism.

Dr Isuwa Dogo, National Publicity Secretary of the Forum, in a statement on Sunday and made available to *New Nigerian*, said that his participation in political emancipation of the country from British colonial powers showed Pa Fasanmi as one of the guiding lights that joined hands with other nationalists to gain political freedom.

The statement observed, "The Elder statesman's active participation in the activities of Nigeria's sociocultural organisations revealed the depth of commitment he had for the emancipation of Nigerians from the claws of injustice made worse by the presence of a system that has continued to render the dreams of the nation's founding fathers impossible to realise."

Ohanaeze Ndigbo, Igbo sociocultural organisation

Igbo sociocultural organisation, Ohanaeze Ndigbo, has described the death of Second Republic Senator, Pa Ayo Fasanmi, as a big blow to Nigeria, saying he died when his counsel was needed most in the nation's march towards democratisation.

In a condolence message by its President-General, Chief John Nwodo, to the family on Friday, Nwodo said, "It is sad that Pa Fasanmi left us now that his counsel was needed most in the nation's march towards democratisation and in its most distressful period. I can recall Senator Ayo Fasanmi's innumerable contributions to nation building as a pharmacist, politician, and elder statesman during his stint as president of the Pharmaceutical Society of Nigeria, member of the Board of Directors of the old Western Nigeria Housing Corporation, and member legislature of Federal Republic of Nigeria.

It is worthy to note that Pa Fasanmi was a humble and selfless leader, and champion of democracy who gave the Yoruba nation a place in Nigerian politics by contributing to the formation and sustenance of Afenifere. As an ardent follower of the great sage, Pa Awolowo, Senator Ayo Fasanmi was consistent in his fight for the downtrodden, epitomised in his immortal statement that "my greatest challenge is ensuring that Awo's legacies do not end.

On behalf of Ohanaeze Ndigbo Worldwide, I condole with the people and government of Osun and Ekiti States, Afenifere and his friends for this irreparable loss.

Most especially, I commiserate with Pa Fasanmi's family and urge them to bear his demise with fortitude and pride because he lived a good, remarkable and fulfilled life during his 94 years sojourn on earth".

South-West All Progressives Congress Caucus

Late Fasanmi Should Be Immortalised
The South-West caucus of the All Progressives Congress (APC) has described the late frontline Afenifere leader, Senator Ayo Fasanmi, as a great Awoist who lived and protected the

political ideology of the late sage, Chief Obafemi Awolowo.

A condolence message signed by its Publicity Secretary, Rt. Hon. Karounwi Oladapo, and made available to journalists in Ado-Ekiti described his demise as a huge loss to the Progressive family in particular and Nigeria as a whole.

It said, "Pa Fasanmi who died at the ripe age of 94 was a very honest and consistent politician who never wavered in his belief in Awolowo's political ideology."

The statement recalled that in spite of old age, the late frontline politician led the campaign for the election of President Muhammadu Buhari first in 2015 and later in 2019.

The Party noted and recognized Senator Ayo Fasanmi's presence on the campaign podium with President Muhammadu Buhari during his re-election campaign in 2019.

He received, campaigned and made powerful speeches in support of President Buhari at the Ekiti Parapo Pavilion, Ado Ekiti, at an advanced age of 93. This was very unique and remarkable! The South-West APC Leaders urged the Federal Government to name a National monument after him, in commemoration and recognition of his innumerable contributions to Democracy, good Governance and National development.

Senator Ayo Fasanmi kept faith and loyalty with the Chief Obafemi Awolowo led Progressive Parties, (Action Group, and Unity Party of Nigeria), the Social Democratic Party, the Action Congress of Nigeria, and lately, the All Progressives Congress. He never deviated from his commitment to the Social Democratic Principles and Progressive ideals until he breathed his last, on Wednesday, July 29, 2020.

He championed the tenets of Afenifere sociopolitical

organisation in its original form, as espoused by Obafemi Awolowo and the Action Group of the First Republic. He never had anything to do with the conservatives and reactionary elements in the Nigerian political space.

Chief Ayo Fasanmi was a Federal House of Representatives member under the Action Group political party of the First Republic, and a distinguished Senator of the Federal Republic of Nigeria, in the Second Republic, between 1979 and 1983.

The party sent its condolences to the family of Senator Fasanmi and the good people of Ekiti State.

Reuben Fasoranti, Afenifere Leader

Farewell to Senator Ayo Fasanmi

On behalf of members of Afenifere, I commiserate with the family of Senator Ayo Fasanmi and the Government and people of Ekiti state on the passing away of the Second Republic Senator.

Senator Ayo Fasanmi will be remembered as a firebrand Action Grouper who distinguished himself as a principled fighter for the ideals of our Leader, Chief Obafemi Awolowo, in the days of siege.

As a UPN Senator in the Second Republic, he was also very distinguished.

His life was meritorious and would always be remembered. May his soul rest in peace.

Afenifere Renewal Group (ARG) Ekiti State Chapter

A Titan goes marching on

We, in the Afenifere Renewal Group (ARG) Ekiti State Chapter, are proud to join millions of people in the burial rites for Pa Ayorinde Fasanmi. But we are no less glad to praise him.

Pa Fasanmi had been so many things to so many of us. He was a great patriot, consummate interlocutor, beloved father, politician's icon, veteran of political battles, devout follower of Awolowo school of thought, and leader of the Afenifere Egbe Ilosiwaju Yoruba. His curriculum vitae is one any credible politician on these shores would be proud of.

To be sure, we were shocked when news of his passing broke. Pa Fasanmi's passing can only be described as death at a ripe old age. In his final months, however, he had been fond of reminding us how he planned to attend his centenary birthday. Occasionally, he would add that he was already preparing to attend some birthday event in honour of some of us or other important ceremonies due many years hence. Even as jokes, these and other similar statements spoke to Pa Fasanmi's self-confidence. We think they point to a man who had done his best on this side of life, and was not afraid of whatever the future might bring with it.

But although Papa didn't die young, his passing is a huge loss to us in ARG, Ekiti State. We would have loved to have him on this side for a little longer. Why? Pa Fasanmi had seen nearly all there was to see in public service in Nigeria. He was a veteran of the important political battles Nigeria had had to fight since late colonial era. He was a repository of knowledge; and he was willing and able to share with others some of the lessons from his long exposure to realpolitik. All of us in ARG, Ekiti State would have loved to share a bit more of the body of knowledge that Pa Fasanmi was.

Moreover, Papa was highly principled. This, some might say, is as noted students of Awolowo School of Politics are wont. Yet, Pa Fasanmi brought on added value. He was quick to identify—and to seize—that fleeting moment when superior argument came on stream, and a shift in this or that prior position had become more useful in the interest of the wider community. He was a politician's politician—if the coinage can be allowed.

Senator Olabiyi Durojaiye, Afenifere Leader

I speak on behalf of fellow members of Afenifere (Egbe Ilosiwaju Yoruba) of which Baba, Distinguished Senator Ayorinde Fasanmi was a committed leader. We are here to say farewell to our amiable, patriotic, and jovial leader whose remains will today, August 4, 2020, be interred in his hometown Iye-Ekiti.

We cannot forget his multiple achievements, as a successful pharmacist, honourable member for Ekiti North in the Federal House of Representatives, and Distinguished Senator during the Second Republic.

He consistently remained in the political "progressive" divide of political thoughts throughout his life. He was a loyal supporter of Chief Obafemi Awolowo—foremost political leader of Yoruba. He was also a colleague and political associate of Senator Abraham Adesanya—the third and immediate past political leader of the Yoruba.

He spent the longer part of his life in Osogbo as a successful pharmacist and community leader. His landmarks in the Church and in the public of two States were remarkable that today the Governments of Ekiti and Osun are playing major roles to honour our veritable leader who, up to last Wednesday, 29th July, 2020 when he breathed his last, was the oldest Senator in the Federal Republic of Nigeria. No wonder the President of the Federal Republic of Nigeria, President Muhammadu Buhari and many other distinguished Nigerians from all over the country have testified and paid glowing tributes to our humble and amiable leader.

Although his amiable wife, Mrs. Felicia Adejoke Fasanmi, predeceased him, Baba Fasanmi was blessed with and succeeded by many good and successful children, one of whom has risen to be a Judge in one of the High Courts of Nigeria.
May his soul rest in peace.

Gani Adams, Aare Onakakanfo of Yorubaland

Aare Onakakanfo of Yorubaland, Iba Gani Adams, has described the death of Pa Ayo Fasanmi, a prominent leader of Pan-Yoruba sociocultural group, Afenifere, as a great loss to Nigeria and the Yoruba nation.

Adams, in a statement by his Media Aide, Kehinde Aderemi, on Thursday in Lagos, said that the Yoruba nation had lost one of her strong voices.

The Aare said the death of the late Fasanmi had created a big vacuum among great leaders of Yoruba race.

"With the exit of the late Pa Ayo Fasanmi, we have lost one of our finest personalities. The death of the Yoruba leader was a great loss to Nigeria and the Yoruba race in particular.

Baba was a great man with an exemplary character. He was so devoted to the cause of our race, and he stood firm during the dark era of the military.

Pa Fasanmi, in his time, loomed larger than that of his peers. He was an epitome of humility, selflessness, and integrity".

According to Adams, there is no doubt that the Yoruba nation will sorely miss his radical approach to issues.

He added that late Pa Fasanmi was an Awoist that impacted his generation.

"He was among the core loyalists of the late Chief Obafemi Awolowo that was reputed to be a strong voice and a symbol of courage."

"He made enviable and remarkable contributions to his profession, to the sociopolitical development of Yorubaland, and to the nation at large," he said.

The late Afenifere leader, Pa Ayo Fasanmi, who died on Wednesday, July 29, aged 94 years, will be buried at his hometown, Iye Ekiti in Ilejemeje Local Government Area of Ekiti State on Tuesday, August 4, 2020.

Yoruba Youth Sociocultural Association (YYSA)

For the Yoruba Youth Sociocultural Association (YYSA) the death of the prominent leader, Senator Ayo Fasanmi remains a monumental loss not only for Yorubaland but Nigeria at large.

The association's secretary, Olawale Ajao, in a statement in Ibadan yesterday stated that Fasanmi was a core progressive and Awoist whose impacts and contributions could not be forgotten.

Iye-Ekiti Youth

Pa Ayorinde Fasanmi was a great blessing to the Community and the entire Ile Yoruba, and Nigeria at large. His lifestyle really touched the life of teeming youths in Iye-Ekiti seriously and we never wanted him to leave us, but of course God wanted him more.

Oba Adeyeye Ogunwusi, OOni of Ife

Afenifere leader, Fasanmi, brought dignity to Yoruba race
The Ooni of Ife, Oba Adeyeye Ogunwusi, Ojaja II, has described the late Afenifere leader, Pa Ayo Fasanmi, as a man of accomplishments, who brought dignity to all descendants of Oduduwa.

This was contained in a tribute signed by his Director of Media and Public Affairs, Moses Olafare, in Ile-Ife.

Ooni Ogunwusi described the late Afenifere leader as an epitome of leadership, politics, and good governance.

"Pa Ayo Fasanmi was a great leader whose words, actions,

and involvement in Nigerian politics brought dignity to the Yoruba people.

He came, he saw, and indeed conquered. The kind of blessings he received is uncommon and God in his infinite mercy crowned it all with a healthy long life filled with prosperity.

We are going to miss him greatly because of the roles he has been playing as an elder statesman.

But we shall continue to remember him for the good he did when he was with us.

Our leaders, particularly those in the political class, have a lot to learn from Pa Fasanmi's selfless style of leadership.

We must wake up to our responsibilities towards creating the great Nigeria of our dreams." the royal father said.

Oba J. Agboola Adeleye-Oni, Oyiyosiye Ilufemiloye Oluwafemiloye I, Oniye of Iye-Ekiti

I, HRM Oba J.A Adeleye-Oni, my Chiefs and the entire Iye-Ekiti community express our appreciation to God for the life well-spent of our illustrious father, Senator Ayo Fasanmi, the Jagun Oshin of Iye-Ekiti. He came, he saw, and he conquered.

Senator Ayo Fasanmi contributed significantly to the progress and development of Iye-Ekiti. The establishment of Ilejemeje High School, provision of electricity and pipe borne water in the community were due to his efforts and those of others.

Politically, he empowered many indigenes of Iye-Ekiti. He was an asset in every way to Iye-Ekiti. He was a progressive politician to the core. He detested dishonesty and corruption. He was an epitome of honesty, integrity and sincerity. His life was full of selfless service to humanity. Forever, Iye-Ekiti shall be grateful to Almighty God for giving us this statesman who has projected the image of Iye-Ekiti to the whole world.

May Baba rest in peace.

I, humbly, wish that the Federal Government of Nigeria, Ekiti State Government, Osun State Government, the Afenifere and Yoruba nation help us immortalise our respected leader by establishing a College of Education, Polytechnic or University here in Iye-Ekiti.

Oba Adekunle A. Adeagbo, Oore Otun-Ekiti

Senator Ayo Fasanmi: A rare gem

One of my living role models, who highly shaped my view on life, work, and many other things, has passed.

You carved your name on hearts, not on tombstones, and your legacy is etched into the minds of others and the stories they share about you continue to rekindle forever.

Father, a bull does not know the value of its tail until it is cut off: so that was what you were to your environment, the Afenifere, and the entire political landscape in Nigeria.

Oba Jimoh Olanipekun Oyetunji, Ataoja of Osogboland

On behalf of HRM, I tender condolences in respect of our Baba Fasanmi who has done so much. Baba was of many parts, he changed so many lives for the better when he was running Bamidupe Chemist at Fagbewesa,. He played a leading role at All Saints' Church, Balogun Agoro, Osogbo before the church became a Cathedral in the Diocese of Osun. Osogbo benefitted immensely when Papa Fasanmi became Senator and Leader of Afenifere.

May God Almighty enable him to rest in perfect peace.

Oba Aderemi Adedapo Adeen, Alayemore of Ido-Osun.

Asiwaju of Ido Osun—Our icon passed on to eternity

Our amiable, Pa (Asiwaju) Senator Ayorinde Fasanmi has shed mortality for immortality, joining his earthly damsel and returning to his Creator.

Going by your remarkable achievements, brilliance, tenacity, and relentless selfless services to humanity with your loyalty to principles, policies and politics of the late revered sage, Chief Obafemi Awolowo, 'till your last breath, you have left your golden footprints in the sands of time.

On your 90th birthday where you gladly accepted to serve as the Asiwaju of our Kingdom, your relentless pursuit of our MKO Abiola International Airport, Ido-Osun with Aregbesola Administration, was profoundly passionately pursued, but the rest is history.

Please continue to rest peacefully in the bosom of your Lord.

Peter Olubowale, Bishop of Ekiti Oke.

Materialism will lead to hell, cleric warns.

In his sermon at Senator Ayo Fasanmi's funeral, the Bishop of Ekiti Oke, Anglican Communion, Reverend Peter Olubowale, said Fasanmi was not a noisemaker and troublemaker during his time, adding that his transition on earth corroborated that "life is not important except it has impacts on others." Olubowale said: "We need to be available to ourselves and be committed to God and set goals. Nigeria is in the position it is today not because we don't have material and human resources, but we lack the commitment to ourselves, set goals, and the welfare of the people. Nigerians are the number one people in the world that are easy to govern. They have patience, zeal, and elastic endurance. When you think they will fall, they will just stand and be looking and I think our political leaders will not play too much on this. Many of us no longer have trust in this nation. No trust in ourselves, no trust in our leaders. Baba has told us that all these monies you are spending and the one you are keeping inside bullion vans and the ones being stashed in bank accounts, all is vanity.

"The suffering in town is much. Use the position you are occupying very well to develop humanity. This is the only way you can gain eternity, the most important reward for all of us because materialism will lead you to hell."

Isaac I. Oluyamo, Bishop Ilesha North Diocese, JP

Human life is like a morning star. It appears brighter in the morning but just for a moment. When affection is most built towards it, it disappears and never comes again.

O! Bringing to mind the saying that at the dawn of day the cock will crow, at a period of time the bell rings. A journey of a thousand year comes to an end one day; when the runners take their rest. A hero has gone to take his eternal rest in the bosom of his Creator.

My relationship with Baba had divine connection; as a young Priest, I was Baba's Vicar at St. John's Anglican Church, Iye-Ekiti, his hometown, and as the Dean of the Cathedral, I was his Vicar at the Cathedral of All Saints' Balogun, Agoro, Osogbo. I was his prayer partner and Bible teacher. To bear witness that he was not just a parishioner, but a father to us, he paid us a visit early this year at the Bishop Court, Ijebu-Jesa, not knowing that he came to bid us farewell.

We bless God for his life well spent. We thank God for his contributions to the growth of the Church and humanity; as a man of timber and calibre, he humbly devoted himself to the service of God and national development. He was a lover of Priests and their families. His huge and tremendous impact in growing life and communities will forever remain fresh in our memory.

The legacy Baba left behind is a confirmation that he lived a fulfilled life, and we are convinced that God will grant him eternal rest.

We will forever miss you, Baba. We pray that your children will enjoy divine grace and honour as they took care of you at old age in Jesus' name. Amen.

May your good work live forever with us and your gentle soul be received into eternal rest.

James A. Popoola, Retired Bishop of Osun Diocese.

Papa Ayo Fasanmi fully surrendered his life to Jesus and served God till he breathed his last.

He loved Osun Diocese so much and built a standard science laboratory for John Mckay Anglican Grammar School Oluode, Osogbo. He also gave generously for the growth of the Cathedral of All Saints Osogbo and the Diocese of Osun.

All Saints Cathedral Church Osogbo

The news of the demise of Papa Fasanmi got to us as a rude shock! A real shock because Papa's voice didn't crack each time we called on him. His smiles and strong voice didn't give a sign of departure. He could sing the various hymns we raised even "off-hand" each time we called on him.

The acronym of his JOY was Jesus first, others next and yourself last. Baba as a Church Chief was a solemn giver. He was God-fearing to a fault.

May your gentle soul rest in peace. We bid you farewell with your favourite hymn: *"Aigbagbo bila! t'emi l'Oluwa, on o si dide fun igbala mi."*

ENDNOTES

[1]James S. Coleman, *Nigeria: Background to Nationalism*, (Berkeley:University of California Press,1958):41-46.

[2]Quoted in Nigeria Tribune editorial, August 14, 2020.

[3]This is a summary of the key points in his contributions in the House of Representatives, and in the Senate. Full statements are in Chapter Two.

[4]Ruth First, *Power in Africa,* (New York: Pantheon Books, 1970); Billy J. Dudley, *An Introduction to Nigerian Government and Politics,* (Macmillan Publishers, 1982):74-124.

[5]Rotimi Suberu, *Federalism and Ethnic Conflict in Nigeria* (Washington D.C.:US Institute for Peace,2001):19-30. An overview of publications on the political history of Nigeria can be found in A. Carl LeVan, *Contemporary Nigerian Politics: Competition in a Time of Transition and Terror* (Cambridge: Cambridge University Press, 2019):14.

Orobola Fasehun holds a Ph.D. in Political Science from Rutgers University, USA with many years of experience in academia and diplomacy.

Olufunmilayo Fasehun earned a Ph.D. from the University of Glasgow, Scotland and has a background in academia, biotechnology and healthcare. She is the daughter of late Senator

ABOUT THE AUTHORS

Orobola Fasehun holds a Ph.D. in Political Science from Rutgers University, USA with many years of experience in academia and diplomacy. He is the author of *A Life in Diplomacy* (2016) and co-authored *OAU After Twenty Years* (1983)

Olufunmilayo Fasehun earned a Ph.D. from the University of Glasgow, Scotland and has a background in academia, biotechnology, and healthcare. She is the daughter of late Senator Ayo Fasanmi.

www.ingramcontent.com/pod-product-compliance
Lightning Source LLC
Chambersburg PA
CBHW060235030426
42335CB00014B/1473